THE CONSCIOUS

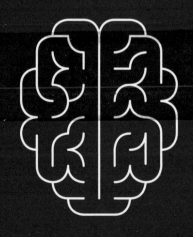

The MIT Press Essential Knowledge Series

THE CONSCIOUS MIND

ZOLTAN L. TOREY

The MIT Press | Cambridge, Massachusetts | London, England

MIT Press books may be purchased at special quantity discounts for business or sales promotional use. For information, please email special_sales@mitpress.mit.edu.

This book was set in Chaparral Pro by the MIT Press. Printed and bound in the United States of America.

Library of Congress Cataloging-in-Publication Data

Torey, Zoltan.
The conscious mind / Zoltan L. Torey.
    pages   cm.—(The MIT Press essential knowledge series)
Includes bibliographical references and index.
ISBN 978-0-262-52710-1 (pbk. : alk. paper)
1. Cognition. 2. Consciousness. 3. Brain. I. Title.
BF311.T6548   2014
153—dc23
2014003649

10   9   8   7   6   5   4   3   2   1

To Margaret Dawn

CONTENTS

SERIES FOREWORD

The MIT Press Essential Knowledge series offers accessible, concise, beautifully produced pocket-size books on topics of current interest. Written by leading thinkers, the books in this series deliver expert overviews of subjects that range from the cultural and the historical to the scientific and the technical.

In today's era of instant information gratification, we have ready access to opinions, rationalizations, and superficial descriptions. Much harder to come by is the foundational knowledge that informs a principled understanding of the world. Essential Knowledge books fill that need. Synthesizing specialized subject matter for nonspecialists and engaging critical topics through fundamentals, each of these compact volumes offers readers a point of access to complex ideas.

Bruce Tidor
Professor of Biological Engineering and Computer Science
Massachusetts Institute of Technology

PREFACE

This book is not an academic monograph. It is, rather, a brief introduction to our understanding of the conscious mind. However, this is probably the only way such an all-encompassing work can be written. This is because to do justice to the controversies of the text's multifaceted subject matter would result in a long and esoteric tome, one that is out of reach for the interested general reader. For this reason I have dispensed with exhaustive presentations of arguments and opted for brevity and accessibility. The result is a model that accounts for the human story, for our breakthrough to language, consciousness, and mind. It is a model that is anchored in all the relevant disciplines and which brings their wisdom into a single focus. I must also stress that what the text aims to outline is not educated guesswork, a "just so" story; far from it. Its credentials are solid. They are anchored to *The Crucible of Consciousness*, my earlier, scholarly work, the carefully crafted offshoot of which this book represents. *The Crucible of Consciousness* was published by Oxford University Press in 1999 and in 2009 by MIT Press with a foreword by Professor Daniel C. Dennett, Director of Cognitive Neuroscience at Tufts University, Medford, Massachusetts.

In this book, I concentrate on what is essential, namely, the identification of the psychic apparatus responsible for our feeling of an inner self, our physical mind, and our sense of free will. Equally important, the text shows why these attributes are opaque to introspection. The reader will recognize that this opacity constitutes a hiatus in our understanding of how the mind works. This hiatus is the niche that all belief systems exploit to explain the world and our place in it. To account for it in technical terms does away with the mystery, replaces fiction with fact, and gives us insight that has personal and cultural significance.

Besides sparing the reader immersion in esoteric controversies, the text documents our emergence as the beings we are today and the underlying changes our species has undergone to make us effective and thought-capable creatures. As for the many experts I have consulted and drawn on in the fields of neuroscience, linguistics, evolutionary biology, and others, the pyramid of knowledge they have amassed is formidable. Without their labors, my work would not have been possible, yet their very specialization prevents them from taking the integrative approach that has been open to me. In conclusion, I am gratified that this volume, *The Conscious Mind*, is part of MIT Press's Essential Knowledge series and can reach an interested and broad readership to shed light on the fascinating and important subject of the human mind.

ACKNOWLEDGMENTS

I want to thank my valued friends, research scientists Dr. Doug Cocks and Dr. Franzi Poldy, who, at the end of an enjoyable brainstorming session, left me with the kernel of an idea. It was to write a concise and accessible work giving a science-based account of human emergence, replacing mythologies with facts but in no way lessening the grandeur of our story. The seed sown, it was a challenge to write this book, its brevity calling for discipline.

Then there are friends whose contribution to the final form of the text was significant. In particular I want to thank David Lenton for his generosity in tirelessly reading for me, Beverley Ranclaud for turning my typescript into computer print and for her unfailing patience with endless changes, Jean Cooney for her labor of love in editing the text, and Syd Hooker for his enthusiastic support and constructive suggestions. In addition I am grateful to the team at MIT Press, especially Philip Laughlin for his encouragement and belief in my work, and Judy Feldmann for her courtesy, efficiency, and creative editorial suggestions. Finally, my wife, Dawn, for all of the above and much, much more: it is to her that I dedicate this book with appreciation, friendship, and love.

INTRODUCTION

An empirical theory of conscious phenomena will not simply waft up out of the neural data. Rather it will be the product of brains that create hypotheses and that creation will draw upon psychology, neuroscience, genetics, computational theory and ethology.

—Patricia S. Churchland, "Brains Wide Shut?" *New Scientist*, April 30, 2005

In an article in the January 2011 issue of *Scientific American* entitled "100 Trillion Connections," the eminent science writer Carl Zimmer had this to say:

A single neuron sits in a petri dish, crackling in lonely contentment. From time to time, it spontaneously unleashes a wave of electric current that travels down its length. If you deliver pulses of electricity to one end of the cell, the neuron may respond with extra spikes of voltage. Bathe the neuron in various transmitters, and you can alter the strength and timing of its electrical waves. On its own, in its dish, the neuron can't do much. But join together 302 neurons and they become a nervous system that can keep the worm *Caenorhabditis elegans* alive—sensing the animal's surroundings, making decisions and issuing commands to the worm's body. Join together 100 billion neurons with 100 trillion connections and you have yourself a human brain capable of much, much more.

How our minds emerge from our flock of neurons remains deeply mysterious. It's a kind of question that neuroscience, for all its triumphs, has been ill equipped to answer. Some neuroscientists dedicate their careers to the workings of individual neurons. Others choose a higher scale: they might, for example, look at how the hippocampus, a cluster of millions of neurons, encodes memories. Others might look at the brain at an even higher scale, observing all the regions that become active when we perform a particular task, such as reading or feeling fear. But few have tried to contemplate the brain on its many scales at once. Their reticence stems, in part, from the sheer scope of the challenge. The interactions between just a few neurons can be a confusing thicket of feedbacks. Add 100 billion more neurons to the problem, and the endeavor turns into a cosmic headache.

This book tackles the emergence of the conscious mind. It shows how the brain acquired self-awareness, functional autonomy,[1] the ability to think, and the ability to understand itself and the world. It is a voyage of discovery, all without causing a cosmic headache.

Some two or three years after the publication of my neuroscience-based interdisciplinary work, *The Crucible of Consciousness*, I began to feel that I had not focused enough on the most intriguing problem of human existence: the nature and the reality of free will and our experience of it. Believing that science is the only road to understanding the world and the way it works, I was troubled by the intractable contradictions free will seems to involve. In a world where every event is lawfully anteceded, caused by what has gone before, there seems to be no room for free volition to elbow in on the proceedings. From this it follows that either we are deluded about being free, or the world we live in is that of "mind–body" dualism, where nonmaterial agencies like causally autonomous minds can play a role and influence outcomes. This is nothing less than a debilitating fault line. Science, unable to account for subjective experience, and the brain, having to fall back on make-believe to make sense, are at a dismal impasse; the challenge is to find the way through.

The volume in your hand suggests a possible solution. It presents an account of the human brain's augmented functioning that underpins the emergent entity, the mind, and throws light on objective facts and subjective experiences alike. It identifies the brain's new "off-line"[2] internal response mechanism, its "second brain" so to speak, with which it accesses itself and then, in combination with brainstem/limbic functions, forms a Darwinian selection mechanism for mentally generated and competing behavioral options. This is a functional breakthrough, one that is impressively straightforward and unexpectedly self-evident. It shows how the animal brain's awareness, its internal representation of the world, became self-accessible and reflective, that is, conscious in the human sense. It shows how protolanguage evolved into language, how a brain subsystem for the emergent mind was built, and why these developments are opaque to introspection. But most importantly, it shows how this new and hitherto unlooked-for and, therefore, undiscovered mechanism furnishes the human brain's emergent mind with the functional autonomy that we experience as free will, yet which is consistent with determinism.

The centerpiece of this writing is the identification of the mind-equipped brain's functional autonomy. I account for its building blocks and specify the part they play in the off-line mechanism's management of the human experience. In the end I hope that the model I am presenting would deserve theoretical physicist John Archibald Wheeler's words from another context, in which he wondered: "How could it have been otherwise? How could we all have been so blind for so long?"

The quest for an interdisciplinary and unifying perspective of knowledge has a distinguished pedigree. Erwin Schrödinger, in his essay "What Is Life?" (1944), first drew attention to its crucial importance for human understanding. This work may then be regarded as the implementation of his program in the mind–brain domain. To quote Schrödinger:

> We have inherited from our forefathers a keen longing for unified and all-embracing knowledge. The very name given to the highest institutions of learning reminds us that from antiquity and throughout many centuries, the universal aspect has been the only one to be given full credit. Yet, the spreading in both width and depth of the multifarious branches of knowledge during the last hundred or so years has confronted us with a dilemma. We feel that we are only now beginning to acquire reliable material for welding together the sum total of all that is known into a whole. On the other hand it has become next to impossible for a single mind fully to command more than a specialized portion of it. I can see no escape from

this dilemma, lest our true aim be lost forever, than that some of us should venture to embark on the synthesis of facts and theories, albeit with second hand and incomplete knowledge of some of them and at the risk of making fools of ourselves.

If this is how matters stood some seventy years ago, how much more acute must the problem be today when, from nuclear physics and brain-imaging to molecular biology, our knowledge grows exponentially while our fields of expertise narrow? Yet, surprisingly, the problem is not so acute. Insights from all fields of scientific endeavors shed new light on old problems and offer an opportunity to answer questions that transcend the confines of individual domains. The unique solution to the human puzzle is something that the individual disciplines of evolutionary biology, neuroscience, and linguistics cannot hope to discover alone, but it is one that the judicial use of their combined database brings well within reach. It was this combined database that enabled me to reconstruct the sequence of events that led to the human breakthrough and reflective consciousness. Drawing on material from these related yet distinct fields allows us to arrive at a model that makes sense of the disparate subjective and objective aspects of the mind–brain domain, revealing their hidden connectedness. The model identifies the conditions that led to the breakthrough that turned *Homo erectus* into *Homo sapiens* and started the chapter of evolution that is dominated by the emergent entity: the human mind. It is the functional autonomy of the human mind that puts us in the driver's seat, confers upon us the agency to codetermine outcomes, and gives neuroscience a human face.

The quest to find the unique solution to the human puzzle—to understand how the system works—is of the greatest importance. Only when viewing ourselves as a whole can we begin to wonder how we might fit into the evolutionary scenario and what insights we might glean about our place in the cosmic process out of which we living entities, "eddies in the stream of entropy,"[3] were so ingeniously generated.

The neurologist and author Oliver Sacks once observed that three mysteries remain to be solved: "How did the universe begin?" "How did life begin?" and "How did consciousness begin?" He then added that the first two might one day be solved, but the third, as to how consciousness began, might have to remain a mystery forever. With reference to this last mystery, the model I am proposing will show that once life began, consciousness too had to emerge. This is because consciousness, just like awareness, its nonreflective animal precursor, is the informational source of the brain's behavioral response. In other words, consciousness is not some newly acquired "quality," "cosmic principle," "circuitry arrangement," or "epiphenomenon," but an indispensable working component of the living system's manner of functioning. It is also likely that, once the universe had begun and the process of complexification was set to run its course, life too, the second of the mysteries, was bound to emerge and progress. This leaves us with the first of these mysteries to contemplate, though with the clarification of mind–brain puzzle, we shall be in a better position than before, when all we had were myths to work with.

In the body of the text, I draw on my earlier work and on the insights and writings of others. A rich and inexhaustible store of knowledge is at my disposal, a bounty for which I am grateful. The book is brief as it deals only with what is essential. It is as accessible as the complexity of the subject matter allows. Its rationale is the Schrödinger program, its validation the accuracy of the model proposed. Its aim is to show the articulations of the jigsaw pieces that solve the puzzle, and its thesis is confirmed by all the disciplines that form its foundation. Let me stress again that the model is not an invention, but a discovery. It is based on the cross-disciplinary linkages that do not always come to the fore in academia, yet if brought together reveal a single perspective that throws light even on specialists' controversies, such as the nature of children's first language acquisition. Echoing Fred Hoyle's (1983) observation that describes the universe as "an inextricable loop where everything exists at the courtesy of everything else," the human organism, too, with all its complexity, is a tightly

Consciousness is not some newly acquired "quality," "cosmic principle," "circuitry arrangement," or "epiphenomenon," but an indispensable working component of the living system's manner of functioning.

consistent system. How it has become what it is is a fascinating story, and this is what this book is about.

A word or two about the plan of this book. The model I am proposing is a single perspective whose aspects interlock and confirm one another. In light of it, I would change only one word in Daniel Dennett's (1991) seminal observation, the observation that prompted me to seek answers that penetrate the layer of conventional understanding:

> The mysteries of the mind have been around for so long and we have made so little progress on them that the likelihood is high that something we all take to be obvious just isn't so.

The word I would change in this thought-provoking passage is *something*, for, as we shall see, most of the things we take to be obvious are wide of the mark. In particular:

• Human consciousness, unlike awareness, is not a unitary phenomenon, but a composite process effect (see chapter 2).

• The mind is neither an ephemeral entity nor brain function writ large, but a sharply delineated neuronal system that is based on language in the conscious brain (see chapter 8).

• Language is not a system of animal communication, but an exclusively human (off-line) brain response, one with which the system guides itself and which makes its awareness reflective (see chapters 3 and 4).

• Syntax[4] is not an intrinsic property of language, but is dictated by the spatiotemporal/causal matrix of the real world that language is constrained to reflect (see chapters 5 and 7).

• The breakthrough from *Homo erectus* to *Homo sapiens* was not a matter of increasing brain size, but one of reorganization in the neotenously regressed and neuroplastic brain of the human infant. It was this reorganization that gave the speech areas the motor abilities and empowered the brain to manage itself (see chapter 3).

• Our sensation of free will is not the work of an entelechy (an uncaused causal agent), but is our conscious awareness of the human mind's active role in the brainstem's[5] decision making (see chapter 10).

• The self is neither a social construct nor an agent that dwells within, but the sense of authorship or agency that the proprioception[6] of speaking or thinking generates (see chapter 11).

• Finally, in chapter 13, I underline that the cosmic system that generated us, the unfolded singularity,[7] constrains us to seek answers that are internal to it.

This, then, is the agenda I shall follow. On the occasion of her last visit to Australia, the renowned anthropologist Margaret Mead was asked what she thought of a then popular book that dealt with the impact on society of a destabilizing future. "The book is worth a chapter," she replied. Having written this unorthodox and densely packed work of not inconsiderable scope, I very much hope that if Mead were asked what she thought of it, she would say: "Every chapter is worth a book."

BACKGROUND TO THE BRAIN: THE IDENTITY OF CONSCIOUSNESS

I have taken the position that there can be no complete science and certainly no science of human beings, until consciousness is explained in biological terms.

—G. M. Edelman, *Bright Air, Brilliant Fire* (1992)

Compared with the sophistication of the knowledge science gives us of the physical world, our understanding of its source—the conscious mind—is dismally lacking. Banished for decades and neglected by neuroscience and psychology alike, consciousness, though still a mystery, is once more a subject of much interest. In this chapter, I clarify its identity by demonstrating its physical substrate. Without such an identification, the breakthrough to *Homo sapiens*, the evolution of language, and the acquisition of our functional autonomy (our sense of free will) cannot be accounted for.

First, much needs to be done to clarify the situation. The terminology is loose; "consciousness" is taken variously to designate "wakefulness," "awareness," "being alive," or "being reflective." It is hard to know what exactly is being referred to in a domain that is described by David Oakley (1985) as "one in which there are as many definitions of awareness or consciousness as there are readers and writers."

It is clear that the related terms "awareness" and "consciousness" are not generally perceived as anchored to identifiable processes in the brain. Although the situation has improved, largely as a result of the sophisticated research in brain-imaging, confusion still persists. For want of real answers, many hold the view that we are self-deluded automata under the control of unconscious processes. As for the impression that we have causal powers, Jeffrey Gray of the London Institute of Psychiatry puts the matter, for him, beyond reasonable doubt: "Consciousness of the stimulus comes too late to affect response" (2004). This is just a polite way of saying that consciousness is an epiphenomenon, a "ghost in the machine" of no relevance to the essentially unconscious organism or the neural processes on which it piggybacks.

Unable to make sense of the term or find a role for it in the workings of the brain, we have simply taken consciousness out of the equation. The result is the so-called hard problem of consciousness, the question of why there is subjective conscious experience over and above the neural information processing that is its substrate. The question remains unanswered, and, if anything, awareness and consciousness are further out of reach than before, when they were subjects of unanchored guesswork.

The problem of what to make of consciousness is ubiquitous; for example, John Searle, in his review of Antonio Damasio's latest work, *Self Comes to Mind* (2010), asks the following questions: "How do neurobiological processes in the brain cause consciousness? How does consciousness function causally in our behaviour?" To answer these, I show the link between neurobiology and consciousness and demonstrate the causal role that consciousness plays in the brain's decision making. To begin, I want to put the biological foundation of awareness and consciousness into the evolutionary context that goes back to the breakthrough from prebiotic complexity to the self-replicating and metabolizing system that is life. While prebiotic complexity and mere animal awareness were fully embedded in the physical world and conformed to the second law of thermodynamics, the law of entropy, consciousness, to use Erwin Schrödinger's words, "stands entropy on its head." It is easy to overlook that this breakthrough divides a causal chain that is until then unbroken, and that life in all its forms is a continuous single event. The breakthrough is an event that unfolds in line with its internal logic and is uniquely dependent on a new and specialized function, that of information processing.

To maintain the organism, to draw on available resources, and, at the same time, to protect the organism from the dangers of the environment was the threefold function of information gathering and processing on which the primitive organism relied. For this purpose, photo-, chemo- and pressure-sensitive spots on the cell evolved to furnish the information required to maintain homeostasis.[1] Information, therefore, was the key to success; the quality of data processing was also significant, and natural selection did the rest. The primitive cell's response was not in any sense problematic. The system was automated and involved no decision making. There was no awareness or consciousness, and information processing went on in the dark; thus the "hard problem" of the conscious mind simply did not arise. However, as we shall see, this halcyon state was nearing its end.

The end came when, in the course of evolution, the single cell-organism was superseded by the multicellular form, and the until then localized and automated information of the sensory spots was "back-relayed" and centrally expressed in nerve nets and later in the specialized organ, the brain. The task of the brain, or at any rate of its sensory side, was the continuous internal representation of what was going on in and around the organism. The representation was a multimodal situation report that the rest of the brain could evaluate and respond to. For the sake of simplicity, I shall refer to this representation as the "endogram," from the Greek *endon* ("inner") and *grammar* ("writing"). It is similar to Vernon Mountcastle's (1979) internal "readout." Importantly, it is the endogram and nothing but the endogram that the animal brain can be aware of and, as we shall see later, which the human brain is conscious of.

First, however, let us look at the changes in the wake of the now centralized information in the endogram. Earlier on, in the single-cell organism, responses were automatic. In the multicellular organism, it became the brain's task to evaluate the stimulus and to select the response that best suited the occasion. This was a "phase-transition,"[2] an evolutionary breakthrough to a higher level of data processing. It involved decision making based on the brain's awareness of the organism's endogram. It must be emphasized that "awareness," and its self-reflective variant "consciousness," are not static entities but ongoing processes. Antonio Damasio (2010) stresses the same point: "Turning processes into things is a mere artefact of our need to communicate complicated ideas to others rapidly and effectively." In an essay entitled "Does Consciousness Exist?" (1904), William James, too, warned against the semantic shift that turns consciousness into an object or attribute. This semantic shift is also relevant for the clarification of the hard problem of consciousness (see chapter 12, "Unfinished Business").

Now, since the term "awareness" refers only to what the brain is aware of (notably the endogram, the sensory

"Awareness" and its self-reflective variant "consciousness" are not static entities but ongoing processes.

totalization) and since the term "consciousness" refers to the endogram's upgraded, self-reflective version, we face a critical distinction. What we are conscious of is no longer just the sensory totalization of the brain, but an augmented product that features the additional output of a new, off-line response mechanism. This mechanism, with its expressive arm of language, generates images and thoughts that are displayed in the endogram, together with the proprioception of their genesis. The hybrid character of the human endogram means that the brainstem is also responding to the off-line mechanism's intracortical contribution. This ingenious neural device enables the brain to modify the nature of its experience and monitor the changes that it itself is in the process of creating. This means that, thanks to the off-line mechanism's contributions, the brainstem's decision making is now qualitatively enriched and the aware state of the brain reflectively conscious.

After the single cell's automated response that did not involve decision making, the centralization of information into an endogram was a breakthrough to awareness and the brain's management of on-line[3] behavior. The era that was dominated by sensory awareness was, however, only the first phase-transition. The acquisition and amazing achievements of the second phase-transition came about as a result of a traceable breakthrough to an internal off-line mechanism (a "second brain," so to speak) that ushered in the era of consciousness; this was the brain's handling of itself and the reflective awareness of what it was doing as it was doing it.

This view of consciousness is confirmed by a passage from Derek Bickerton (1995), in which he illustrates the functional difference between awareness (the purely sensory endogram of the animal brain) and human consciousness, the beneficiary of a neuroanatomical circuitry modification (see chapter 3). Note that Bickerton speaks of "consciousness 1" and "consciousness 2," rather than of "awareness" and "consciousness," which makes a better contrast between the nonreflective and reflective versions of the totalized information, the endogram:

> All creatures, ourselves included, enjoy "consciousness 1," awareness of ourselves and our surroundings to a widely varying degree of richness, poorly in simple organisms, quite thoroughly in some of the more complex ones. However, "consciousness 1" is an "on-line" operation, unceasingly involved in the moment to moment exigencies of existence. "Consciousness 2," consciousness of one's own consciousness, can come only in a species, some of whose brain areas are exempt from this immediate environmental traffic and can scan the behavior of areas of primary consciousness as objectively as the latter scans the environment.

Before I outline the consequences of the off-line mechanism for behavior and the brain's relationship to itself, it is useful to elaborate on the shift in balance between cortex and brainstem that underpins the human brain's functional autonomy.

The difference between what the brain was and what it became is spectacular. Contrasting the 302 neurons of the roundworm with the 100 billion of the human brain, to say nothing of the countless trillions of interconnections that complete the network, reveals the importance of data processing for the organism. Representing about 2 percent of our average body weight, the human brain burns up to 20 percent of the body's total energy output. Nor was its expansion over evolutionary times only quantitative. Most of the cortical areas are specialized to perform highly sophisticated sensory or motor functions. The occipital lobes process vision and aspects of it; the parietal lobes deal with somatic matters such as body image, sensation, and orientation; the temporal lobes specialize in hearing and aspects of speech; and the junctional areas between the lobes deal with ideas and representations of overlapping significance. Deeper in the cerebrum, close to the brainstem and on the inner surfaces of the hemispheres, the limbic areas deal with memory and emotions, vital aspects for the management of life. Forming networks and systems of interaction, it is this sensory side of the brain that totalizes the endogram, the situation report for the brainstem to evaluate and pass on to motor response.

The motor areas that implement the organism's responses are to be found in the frontal lobes, which in the human brain represent some 28 percent of the cortical mass. This figure far exceeds that found in all other species and underlines the importance of the frontal lobes. Anterior to the motor cortices, the prefrontal areas are in charge of our highest functions, our thinking, our reflecting, and orchestrating of the brain's activity as a whole. Significantly, the prefrontal cortices are linked up with all the other areas of the brain and can draw on arousal energy from the reticular formation of the brainstem.

Situated functionally between the sensory side and the motor side of the brain is the organism's decision-making center: the brainstem. This is the home of biological values and of the apportioning of reticular activation for those motor responses it senses to be in the organism's interest.

Turning to the massively altered balance between the cortex and the brainstem, it is significant that, over evolutionary time, the brainstem has altered little. All the refinements of perception, cognition, and data processing were brought about through the expansion, refinement, and specialization of the cortical areas. While these refinements have meant a tremendous boost to the organism's cognitive powers, the brainstem's motor response has remained instinctual as before. In the infrahuman context, the discrepancy between the cortex and the brainstem was minimal and mattered little. By contrast, once we have an off-line mechanism that generates language and mental alternatives, a new situation arises. It involves the awareness of self-created choice that changes the role of the cortex vis-à-vis the brainstem. This off-line mechanism has become an active player in a Darwinian selection, where mental alternatives are run past the brainstem, which then makes the selection.

Damasio (2010) rightly notes that "before consciousness, life's regulation was entirely automated. After consciousness began, life's regulation retains its automation but gradually comes under the influence of self-oriented deliberations." The passage highlights the situation prior to the breakthrough to awareness, when the automated response was all there was, information was not yet uncoupled from response, and decision-making brains did not exist. In terms of my model, which is predicated on not one but two phase-transitions, it is awareness, the product of the first breakthrough, rather than consciousness, the product of the second breakthrough, that Damasio has in mind. This is because consciousness, that is, the ability to "be conscious of," involves reflection, the function of the "off-line" mechanism, which is an evolutionarily late and uniquely human acquisition.

I now return to the changes in human evolution for which the off-line mechanism is responsible. Bickerton's description (cited earlier) is clear and accurate. Reflective human consciousness is the product of a mechanism that does not exist in the animal brain. The mechanism is off-line, as it is not directly involved in what Bickerton calls "environmental traffic," but is able to guide it, modulate it, and substitute for it. Its motor-arm is language, and its products are images and thoughts that are displayed in the endogram and which bring on the attentional oscillation between what is said or thought and the sensation of saying or thinking it (more on this below).

The task now is to show that language enables the brain to respond in two different ways—either by letting the on-line mechanism respond as before or by redirecting or even canceling a would-be response. The presence of a second (internal) mechanism to handle the first is added experience for the brain. The images and thoughts the new mechanism generates form a class of internal saliences.[4] These saliences are featured together with the sensory saliences in an endogram that is no longer "flat" and inaccessible to the brain but "layered" and easily managed by the off-line mechanism from within.

The evolutionary and functional significance of the endogram having become layered and therefore accessible to internal handling is enormous. Whereas in the past the brain had no choice but to attend to the dominant salience of the moment—say, a loud noise, or the sighting of a predator or of a prospective mate—it is now able to switch its attention to any of the saliences in its layered endogram, including those that it itself is generating. This switch is possible now because language is under voluntary muscle control and can direct the organism's attention as required. Yet there is more to this new dispensation than attentional motility. Every response we make with speech or thought to any of the saliences in our endogram invariably brings on a companion or cosalience generated by the proprioception of the utterance. This cosalience is the sense of a self or agency that we feel whenever we speak or think. It makes us aware that we are inextricably a part of what we are conscious of. It also explains why the experience of a salience plus its generative source (the proprioception of the utterance) brings on an attentional oscillation between them, making us conscious of what we are saying and that *we* are saying it. Human consciousness is, therefore, double stranded: it features the subject, that is, the salience that is in focus, together with the cosalience, that is, the self-created sense of agency that accompanies it.

What I have just outlined is evolution's ingenious way of turning the inaccessible and purely on-line animal brain into an active player in the charting of its behavioral course. By selecting and managing a mix of saliences, the conscious mind brings about the stimulus configuration that the brainstem has to attend and respond to. It is, then, through this "stacking of the cards" that the language-equipped brain becomes the source of its own causal leverage and of the motility of thought that is needed for insight and for functioning as a self-guiding system.

The purpose of this chapter is to clear up any confusion about the identity of awareness and of consciousness, to show how they were generated to play a causal role in the brain's processing of information. Beyond the single-cell level, we have identified two phase-transitions. The first is a transition to awareness, the second to consciousness; the latter involves an off-line mechanism for the brain to handle itself and to manage its on-line behavior. The way this is done is detailed in chapter 8, in connection with Benjamin Libet's (1990) "time-on" theory of neural processing. Libet's work corroborates the model of stepwise upgrading that I am proposing. My model shows that human consciousness is a neurobiological process and not an ephemeral quality as some believe. The changes that underpin reflective human functioning were gradual, but once the speech areas had acquired a motor-arm, the evolution of language and of a conscious self in charge of it was an inevitable consequence.

Note that the intriguing phenomena of consciousness, self, mind, and free will have been the subject of much ingenious speculation and erudite debate, especially in the domains of philosophy and the philosophy of mind. A vast literature bears witness to this, yet the debate remains unresolved. This is because the neural process that generates these phenomena lies outside the reach of these disciplines, and also because the phenomena are regarded as entities in their own right, when they are in fact mere aspects of the same underlying process. It is this process and the way the above phenomena are interrelated that the proposed model is designed to clarify. In the coming chapters, I account for the pieces of the puzzle and for evolution's ingenious way of achieving functional autonomy for the human mind.

The trajectory of life's evolution from the first cell to the functionally autonomous human mind is an awe-inspiring saga. Only at a few critical points are there still problems that await solution. The question of how, out of the prebiotic soup, self-replicating life could emerge is particularly challenging; one answer is that life came about through an interlocked and increasingly stable set of auto-catalytic cycles,[6] a stepwise progression rather than a single leap. This view accords with George Porter's (1971) observation: "The lottery for the inception of life may well have been played with loaded dice at every stage of a graduated sequence."

More accessible are the circumstances that led to the breakthrough to *Homo sapiens* and gave birth to a brain that is the codeterminant of outcomes. Yet even here, with relevant data on hand, how the breakthrough could have occurred is unclear. The paucity of modeling and the narrow focus of expertise are in part to blame. Of course, it is unrealistic to expect that any of the disciplines concerned with our human emergence could solve this complicated interdisciplinary puzzle alone. Furthermore, guesswork gets us nowhere, while the claim that consciousness is an epiphenomenon without causal relevance speaks only of ignorance of how the brain works. Then there is simple introspection, though it too will be shown to hinder the search for insight and to be a source of serious misconstructions.

Having specified the purpose of this writing as the identification and evolution of the autonomous human brain, we can now begin to trace its emergence. It is a success story of great significance. It started with the second phase-transition that put us in the driver's seat, giving us agency, a passport to knowledge, mastery, and insight into the nature of the biological and physical world.

NEOTENY: THE BREAKING OF THE HOMINID IMPASSE

It is quite senseless to raise the problem of explaining the evolution of language from more primitive systems of communication.

—Noam Chomsky, *Language and Mind* (1968)

The acquisition of an off-line mechanism (a brain within the brain) with language as its motor-arm was an evolutionary breakthrough, the key to the transformation of *Homo erectus* into *Homo sapiens* and to the quantum leap in processing efficiency that changed the brain's relationship to itself. In this chapter, I suggest a likely explanation of how it all came about and how the foundation for language evolution was put in place.

The search for the critical factor that set off the chain of events typically focuses on the examination of systems of animal communication as forerunners of human language. Reflecting on this approach, Derek Bickerton in his work *Adam's Tongue* (2009) cites Chomsky as saying:

> It is almost universally taken for granted that there exists a problem of explaining the evolution of human language from systems of animal communication. However, the studies of animal communication only serve to indicate the extent to which language appears to be a unique phenomenon without significant analog in the animal world.

If we compare human language with animal communication, we find that they are not on the same developmental continuum but are different in kind. Human language is subserved by a dedicated (off-line) neural circuit that is lateralized to the left brain. Its output is displayed in the endogram and can significantly modify the organism's behavior. It uses word-labeled percepts[1] to generate statements that are context independent and may be used to affect the decision-making process of the brain. In other words, it is a device of "cognitive bootstrapping" with which the brain can guide itself. If the dedicated circuit is damaged, the speech skill is impaired and can even be lost.

By contrast, what we call animal communication, say, the vervet monkey's three distinct warning calls, is an on-line behavior. It does not involve circuitry modifications of any kind or a dedicated response mechanism that the

If we compare human language with animal communication, we find that they are not on the same developmental continuum but are different in kind.

brain can use out of context and at its own discretion. Animal communication, whether of the vocal, gestural, or body-language variety, is always part of the organism's total response. It cannot be used as a signaling implement out of context or in the absence of the feeling or hormone-driven disposition that brings it on. By contrast with the neural vulnerability of lateralized human language, the splitting of the infrahuman brain does not affect its signaling, because animal communication is not a specialized cognitive skill.

If human language, the expressive arm of an entirely new brain mechanism, is not animal communication writ large, then what is its foundation? There is, of course, the spectacular expansion of the hominid brain. The primate branch that became the human line goes back to *Australopithecus*. Already bipedal, with a brain that was lateralized in the ratio of 4 to 1 in favor of the right hand (as is the case with us), *Australopithecus* had a brain capacity slightly above that of the chimpanzee. Over the next four to five million years it was this hominid line that evolved, increasing in body size, but even more in brain size to exceed the 750 cubic centimeters (ccs) capacity (estimated by Phillip Tobias [1971] and others) as the minimum requirement for some rudimentary protolinguistic communication. Following *Homo habilis*, the first tool-user, *Homo erectus*, our immediate precursor, took center stage. Though it mastered the art of fire and had a brain capacity of about 1,000 ccs, enough for some form of language development, an amazingly long period of total stagnation followed. Puzzling over this, Bickerton (2009) expressed his amazement in the form of a rhetorical question:

> Couldn't the predecessors of our modern humans have done just a little better than the million years of the same old hand axe? Couldn't they have done something to break what one paleo-anthropologist referred to as "the almost unimaginable monotony" of the Lower Paleolithic, the Old Stone Age?

The answer is clear, as is the reason for it. Brain expansion as such had run its course, had reached the optimal level of on-line processing, and had nowhere to go. Something new, something different had to occur to break the impasse, to open the brain up to itself by evolving an additional, internal (off-line) response mechanism, one able to guide and control the brain's output and to do this in an entirely novel way. The additional mechanism was, of course, language, the remarkable acquisition of which we must now explore.

The breakthrough from *erectus* to *sapiens* was brought about by neoteny, evolution's ingenious mechanism to find the way out of the hominid impasse and to give the brain the circuitry modification for autonomous functioning. While bipedalism (which freed the hands for object manipulation) and the group context of hominid existence were important conditions, it was the neotenous regression of the brain's neural maturation, with its cognitive consequences, that was selected for, not some form of animal communication as has been widely believed. It was through neoteny that brain plasticity at the right developmental stage could bring about the critical rewiring of the left brain, the step that led to syntactic language and the achievement of self-reflective consciousness.

Neotenous regression, the tendency to start out postnatal life in a less mature state than did our ancestors, shifts the emphasis from instincts to learning process as the dominant factor in the acquisition of the organism's survival and coping skills. This is how Stephen J. Gould (1977) describes the process:

> Animals become too committed to the peculiarities of their environment by evolving a fine-tuned design for a highly specific mode of life. They sacrifice plasticity for future change. Neoteny can now come to the rescue and provide an escape from specialization. Animals can slough off their highly specialized adult form, return to the lability of youth and prepare themselves for new evolutionary directions.

How, then, did neoteny work to bring on the critical change to the human brain? To answer this, I turn to the respective growth curves that represent the brain development of the young *erectus* and the young *sapiens*. Unsurprisingly, the two curves show a tremendous difference in the respective age levels at which the brain size necessary for language development is reached. For the young *erectus*, the critical age was six, whereas for the *sapiens* infant it is one. It is not hard to see that by the time the *erectus* had enough neurons to make some, even if limited, use of protolinguistic elements such as verbal pointing (naming), its nonlanguage related motor-skills were well established and there was neither the need nor the neuroplasticity to justify a switch.

By contrast, the *sapiens* infant reached the critical stage at the age of one. Without motor skills to draw on and, therefore, having to depend on caregivers, its neuroplastic brain was ideally placed to make use of the vocal medium. It could in fact manipulate, interact with, and, to some extent, control persons and aspects of its environment. Detlev Ploog (1979) puts it this way: "By crying and early modifications of crying they bring their caretakers close and thereby manipulate the environment through their activity."

The infant's physical dependence, developmental stage, and neuroplasticity jointly ensured the successful wiring-in of the vocal skill as an effective means for interpersonal transactions and, later, for language-assisted operations. Now, since all the cortical structures that were involved in the new manipulative medium were receiving increased blood, glucose, and oxygen supply, neural arborization,[2] which depends on such increments, was also facilitated. As a result, protolinguistic and later language operations grew ever more feasible and important for adjustment and breeding selection.

What I am describing here is only the inception and the underpinning of the off-line way of responding. The key event that set in motion the cascade of changes that led to *Homo sapiens* was the acquisition of a motor-arm by the speech areas. In the neuroplastic and incompletely wired-up brain of the human infant, more precocious structures can annex and wire up for their own use structures that mature more slowly. It was in this manner, and is still in this manner, that the left frontal motor areas for the handling of objects in space are taken over for the manipulation of verbal objects (words) in inner space. Importantly, the establishment of this vital motor link for speech is a modification that has to be achieved by each and every human brain, and it must happen within a limited time. If this point is passed without the child's brain being given the stimulating opportunity to wire up for verbal control of the environment, the window for acquiring the skill closes and the off-line mechanism that manages speech and thought fails to appear.

The redeployment of left-hemispheric manipulo-spatiality[3] to serve as the motor-arm of language leaves the brain's object manipulation in the hands of its right-hemispheric analogue. The close association of speech and gesticulation bears witness to their respective sources in the original sister functions. Confirming the source of the speech skill in the structures just identified, Michael Gazzaniga and Joseph Le Doux (1978) noted that "it is clear that manipulo-spatiality and language are complexly related. Manipulo-spatial abilities may have provided the basis of primitive language (object naming) and both language and manipulo-spatiality require similar neural mechanisms."

The picture of the evolution of language now emerges. The condition of neotenous regression and neuroplasticity led to the wiring for language of the human infant's brain. In other words, it was a change in design, a technical tweak, that broke the cognitive drought, put an end to the long stagnation of *Homo erectus*, and ushered in the era of high-quality internal response management.

The language instrument that did this took some time to evolve. I shall trace its trajectory stage by stage. At the outset there was a tentative, short list of lexical items, bereft of articulating power and without syntax. Yet it was a foothold in an enormously promising and colonizable world, the world we call "mind."

To have a linguistic motor-arm enabled the brain to utter words and so to access and re-expose them to frontal scanning.[4] It also empowered it to switch the attention mechanism from salience to salience, including those saliences it itself was generating, and to sense that it was an active player in managing its experience. The way this protostage evolved to become an accurate instrument for generating syntax and representing the world is a remarkable story, which I recount in chapter 5.

Before closing this chapter, I want to digress and allude to a rather common misperception that the child's acquisition of its first language is a process that requires an intrapsychic scaffold or template. Some linguists and philosophers of mind (for example, Jerry Fodor and Steven Pinker) have proposed hypothetical constructs such as "mentalese," a "language of thought," and the "language instinct" for this purpose. As the coming chapters will show, the process of language acquisition is in fact sufficient unto itself. The acquisition of a motor-arm by the neuroplastic brain of the human infant opens up a new off-line response capability, and it is in the rewarding confines of this that the child's language skill is built. Using its dedicated motor-arm, the child is able to think, that is, to its express thoughts and so be an active player in shaping its inner world and guiding its response. Language, the instrument of reflection and communication, uncouples the brain from having to respond in an on-line fashion and opens up for it the world of the mind.

We can now go on to look at the semantic raw material, the protowords the brain had to work with in the process of building its cognitive tool, the fully fledged language instrument.

THE NUTS AND BOLTS OF LANGUAGE

To me it seems that our current research is not hampered significantly by the lack of accurate data, but rather by an inability to explain in a satisfactory way data that are hardly in question.

—Noam Chomsky, *Language and Mind* (1968)

Having identified the breakthrough from *erectus* to *sapiens*, namely, the acquisition of the dedicated motor-arm for verbalization and speech, we look at the three things that the human brain could begin to work on and with. These were: a handful of vocal signals that were brought across the divide from *Homo erectus*; an ability to name, reiterate, and reexperience at will, courtesy of the recently acquired motor-link; and an accompanying vague but persistent sense of being the source of the experience. This is not much, perhaps, but it was all that was needed to get the ball rolling.

The modular unit of what was to be the basis for speech and self-directed thought was the "word-percept." Since percepts are private, first-person experiences, they cannot be accessed, handled, or communicated without a carrier. The carrier is the word, the sound-pattern with which the brain can bring into circulation and renewed attentional focus its otherwise inaccessible modality experiences (sights, sounds, feelings, and the like).

The words and the percepts they signify are mutually evocative. Uttering the word brings the percept, the modality experience, to mind, just as the experience of a percept calls up the word with which it is linked. It is the word that empowers the brain to dip into its store of images and in so doing generate mental experiences. These in turn enrich the human endogram, which then becomes a living record of its own ongoing contribution to and reflections on itself and the world.

However, to have a workable word-percept bond, both sides of the linkage must be stable and ready to interact. On the word side, this is easy. Phonemic patterns are simple to learn and to hold invariant. Merlin Donald (1991) notes that "our speech sounds are reified. It is as if they were objects or events." On the percept side of the linkage, the matter is more complicated. Prespeech perception, lacking the stabilizing effect of words, was fluid, transient, and without fixed features for bonding. The only aspect of perception that could be used for the purpose was the "constancy mechanism," because its products have the stability and the temporal duration that the linkage with words requires. The constancy mechanism is a remarkable neural device that computes all manner of transformations that objects of attention can undergo. It compensates for apparent changes in size, shape, angle, tilt, twist, distance, or illumination, while the object in focus is experienced as invariant. In this manner, moving objects, faces, and targets in motion can be held in focus and responded to as to unchanging and self-same entities. In the human brain's language-building activity, this neurofunctionally sustained permanence was the source of the initial protovocabulary.

Identifying the percept material that the constancy mechanism was able to stabilize for word linkage is highly significant. This was the material that constituted the protolexicon, which in turn was the springboard for language building. Since the constancy mechanism was furnishing the brain with transforms of objects and actions, the protovocabulary to arise out of this had to consist of nouns and verbs, that is, the lexical categories that stood for them. The manner in which the brain generates and articulates a syntactically sound language out of this limited protostock will be the subject of the next chapter. Here I want to explore the consequences of the brain's newly acquired power of reiteration on the protowords and on the language-based character of the reality that was generated.

The feature I want to look at is what Konrad Lorenz (1978) referred to as "objectification."[1] Because of its stabilizing word linkage, the objectified percept represented a novel phenomenon. It was a hybridized entity that, though perceptlike in its modality (visual, somatosensory, etc.), was in fact constrained by corrective distortions. Yet, and paradoxically, it was precisely these distortions that rendered it suitable for its role in the brain's language-based experience.

The way corrective distortions work is best illustrated by the experimental neurosis paradigm. In this, the experimental subject, a dog, learns to associate the figure of a circle with a food reward and the figure of an ellipse with an electric shock. Next, the circle presentations are increasingly flattened to approximate an ellipse, while the ellipse presentations get gradually rounded out to approximate a circle. Neurotic breakdown occurs when the dog is unable to discriminate and to decide whether the perceived figure is a circle or an ellipse.

What is of interest to us is the dog's ability to keep seeing the increasingly deviant presentations as if they were the original circle and ellipse. It is able to do this by systematically correcting for the perceived deviations, that is to say, by applying accommodating counterdistortions to shore up the deteriorating match. It is this neural technique that enables it to prolong and preserve the functional integrity of the learned stimulus-to-response connection.

In the same way and for the same reason of conserving response integrity, we humans too perceive objects in a way that allows us to go on functioning with socially acquired and objectified images. Our incoming impressions, the things we perceive, are, therefore, subjected to corrective distortions in normative ways. For example, we are programmed to perceive the four-legged object we sit on either as a chair or a stool, depending on the presence or absence of a backrest. The hypothetical hybrid, the one with a very low backrest, we automatically lump into one or the other of the defining categories. It is as if we are obliged to think of the hybrid object either in terms of the class-concept "chair" or the class-concept "stool" and have no choice but to perceive it in one or the other of these preset ways.

This preset and objectified character of our perceived world is, then, the precondition of our word-assisted handling of it. Corrective distortions are essential for our functioning. They enable us to hold onto words and the percepts they signify. Without the fixedness they provide, we would be swamped by the fluidity and the spatiotemporal uniqueness of all that surrounds us. To put it another way, our ability to access percepts through words brings about a cognitively stabilized world of representations, which, though distorted, empowers us to speak and think.

Returning to the beginning of this chapter, it is necessary to ask what kind of a world early *Homo sapiens* found

Our ability to access percepts through words brings about a cognitively stabilized world of representations, which, though distorted, empowers us to speak and think.

on the human side of the divide. Since they could name objects but could not yet form sentences, all they were able to experience were single percepts (nouns and verbs) plus the feeling of a "self" or "authorship" that the proprioception of uttering words generated. At that early stage of protolinguistic development, the world of *Homo sapiens* was word seeded, but the seeds were not linked or articulated: large areas of experience could not be accessed and represented, let alone handled by speech or thought. It was a limited world, yet an excellent launching pad for the colonization of inner space and for the building of a language instrument able to generate the verbal rendition of the full range of human experience. In the coming chapter I shall account for the brain's conquest of this representational space and for the emergence of articulated language, the instrument that empowered it to think and put it firmly and finally in the driver's seat.

COGNITIVE BOOTSTRAPPING: THE EPIGENESIS OF LANGUAGE

Characterizing human language by its construction, linguists constantly treat the atomic units in our speech, either the words themselves or the concepts for which they stand, as if they already existed, ready-made and in advance of speech.

—Jacob Bronowski, *A Sense of the Future* (1977)

The epigenesis[1] of our highly articulated human language is a fascinating story. It begins simply, with the acquisition of a motor-arm for Broca's area[2] and the ability to name percepts generating nouns and verbs. Then, by scanning this protomaterial, the brain extracted a secondary vocabulary (adjectives, adverbs, and function words) that enabled it to achieve syntax.

Going back to where it all started, we want to know what the protolanguage of nouns and verbs was like and what adaptive pressures for upgrading it were in force. The reconstruction of this early stage is not problematic. The language that could be generated at the time could not have been more than a blunt and ambiguity-ridden device. This is because the constancy mechanism, the source of the protovocabulary, could not have created more than a limited stock of nouns and verbs, signifying objects like man, tree, bird, fire, and dog, or actions, like eat, run, sleep, and kill. Such a stock could not have given rise to more than a terse, grammarless, and inarticulate "Tarzan-talk" of the "man eat," "dog sleep" variety.

Complete communication was not possible, as nouns and verbs alone can convey no more than the skeletal outlines of a message. Aspects like qualifying or specifying of events, place, manner, and time cannot even be considered. Without being able to ask who, where, why, when, which, what, or how, no fine-tuning is possible and true communication, the sharing of information by brains, is out of the question.

Such shortcomings notwithstanding, the mere ability to name and to name at will was a marked improvement on what had gone before. It was also an invaluable baseline for the developments that would follow. The ability to switch the attention to and fro between saliences (and whether these were sensory or self-generated) made the brain an active, even if at first clumsy, player on the plane of self-management. It also stimulated neural growth in the brain of the infant, growth that was needed for the upkeep and the expansion of the practice.

Underpinning the significance of this point, Eric Lenneberg (1967) observed:

> The major change that evidently occurs during the expansion of the brain is in the interconnection of cells. Processes grow out of cell-bodies, axons and dendrites, eventually to form a dense network of interconnecting branches. In fact thousands of such offshoots per neuron make their appearance and complete the wiring of the system.

What is important is that this branching development is the brain's response to the demand that tasks be performed. The extent of this collateral branching is, therefore, a function of use. It confers something like weighted advantage on the brain-user and can lead to appreciable differences in effectiveness, even if two brains had been quite comparable to begin with.

How then did "Tarzan-talk" evolve into articulated language, and how were the adjectives, adverbs, and function words generated that were instrumental in achieving syntax? The answer lies with the repeated and massive exposures of the word-linked percepts to the brain's frontal scanning, which led to the extraction of the feature-components that were embedded in them. Word-linked percepts (nouns and verbs) were composite entities that could be broken down into their constituent aspects. The many hundreds, if not thousands, of repeated exposures of these word-linked percepts to frontal scanning were bound to lead to the identification of feature categories, such as color, contour, contrast, texture, form, angle, position, mood, intent, manner, style, and many more.

Once extracted, these categories could be labeled and added to the expanding lexicon as adjectives and adverbs with which to qualify the nouns and the verbs to match the required specifications. To illustrate the secondary, derivative character of these newly extracted word categories, consider that without a noun or a verb to qualify, they make no sense. To call something "tall," "angry," or "fast" demands a subject to qualify, even as the "grin" is nonsensical without the Cheshire Cat. Once an object or action was word-labeled (named), the motor-arm of the speech areas could bring it into repeated circulation and the extraction of the embedded feature-components could begin. Note here that just as population invariants can be extracted from a sample of many instances, invariant aspects embedded in single events or entities can be isolated by the repeated scanning of a sample of one. The scanning of the single event is particularly useful where relative shifts occur. This is the case, for example, when salient data about facial expressions are detected that yield informationally loaded superimpositions, such as changes in mood or intention that can be judged against the basic pattern of a given face.

The work is done here by feature detectors as they filter the output of the scanning brain. Underpinning the view that this was the way the secondary lexicon of adjectives and adverbs was acquired and built into language by early *Homo sapiens*, Colin Blakemore (1978) had this to say:

> Our present view of visual analysis is then that it proceeds as the selective extraction of component features, or points of high informational content on the complete retinal image. It is this decomposition of the visual scene, not into any simple geometric description but into coordinates of a feature-space, whose many axes are inscribed in different and independent regions of the brain.

The picture is clear. Just as the protovocabulary was the product of the constancy mechanism, the secondary lexicon was extracted from the protomaterial through visual analysis. The adjectives, adverbs, and function words thus generated were then deployed to synthesize articulated human language.

The available data indicate a two-stage model of language evolution. The model shows why the secondary vocabulary (including function words) could not have come about without the protomaterial of the nouns and the verbs. This is because the detection and the extraction of embedded features could begin only after the protomaterial was established and its scanning could commence. Once the brain had assembled enough of the components and subcomponents to articulate them into statements, it had a language instrument at its disposal. By arranging the elements in purposive ways, the brain was able to generate the linguistic representations that accurately reflected the spatiotemporal and causal character of the world in which it is embedded.

There is an important point here for us to consider. Contrary to the traditional view that language is the generative source of syntax, it is rather the template of reality, the way the world is, that an evolving language had to reflect. In other words, it is the way objects and events are connected out there in the world that defines what language, every language, must deliver, what its grammar must codify, or else it will fail as a vehicle of communication. This is why there are no failed or half-complete languages, why pidgin turns to Creole in one generation and Creole evolves into a fully fledged language in a short time. The conditions to be mirrored can be met in a number of ways, of course, but the template of reality, the source of syntax, is always the same.

Once the motor-arm for speech was acquired and the constancy mechanism had laid in a modest set of nouns and verbs, the growth of language was an epigenetic process that unfolded from within to colonize and match the requirements of the terrain, human as well as physical. It was guided by feedback mechanisms and environmental confirmations. The two-stage evolution of language finds confirmation when the speech skill deteriorates as a result of lesion or disease and its functional layers, its stages, are shed in the reverse order of their acquisition, leaving the noun, the most primitive component, to be lost last.

Adding weight to the thesis of the stage-wise evolution of language, Bickerton (1995) noted that

the linguistic history of the hominid line appears ... as a two-stage process: first a stage in which there was a lexicon without syntax, then a stage in which infinitely productive mechanisms emerged to create syntax as we know it. If this conclusion is correct, it is a waste of time to look for antecedents of syntax in ancestral species, as syntax could not have come into existence until there was a sizeable vocabulary whose units could be organized into complex structures.
... There seems no feasible alternative to concluding that syntax has a specific neural substrate, laid down at some stage prior to the last fifty millennia, most probably at the time when anatomically modern humans emerged as a separate species.

Bickerton's description is spot on, though it does not say what the "infinitely productive mechanisms" and the "specific neural substrate" for generating syntax actually were. To find these, we turn to the motor writing of the speech areas in the human infant's neuroplastic brain, the breakthrough that gave it the leverage to handle its lexicon and generate syntax when, through feature-detection, it acquired qualifiers and function words.

Once the pieces were to hand, language was a foregone conclusion. The natural frame for this construction work was the sentence, the extended form of the percept. It furnished the temporal space for the qualifying insertions that modify the noun and define its character, activity, and context. The ability to name, to call out the word "dog" and to draw attention to it, enables the brain to specify many things about the dog. It can tell whose dog it is, what sort of dog it is, what it is doing, where, why, and how, and with what result. The sentence is ideal for achieving a good match between nonverbal (modality) experience (sight, sound, etc.) and its linguistic rendition. Adding a pinch or two of qualifying words to the semantic brew sharpens the focus of language, the technique of handling and conveying information. If uttered in communication with others, words become "speech"; if they are rendered internally for one's own contemplation, they are "thought." Thanks to the off-line mechanism's motor control of percepts, the brain is able to manage itself and also, by way of the

The ability to name, to call out the word "dog" and to draw attention to it, enables the brain to specify many things about the dog.

proprioception its activity generates, to know that it is the source of the experience.

As we have seen, the epigenetic build-up of language involved the extraction of secondary features and the means of articulating them. So it was through the secondary material that we came upon the "Aladdin's Cave" of communicational treasures and the facility to achieve syntax, the key to language. The formerly unaskable questions of who, where, why, when, which, what, and how could now be answered, and "Tarzan-talk" could be replaced with articulate speech. The ability to combine word percepts to form sentences and to modulate them "in flight" makes the conveying of information possible and the communication of meaning a rewarding and feasible process.

In summary, the developmental infrastructure of a living language is a rich quarry of information about its stage-wise genesis and the neural substrate responsible for it. The identification of the individual steps that transformed *erectus* into *sapiens* is straightforward. The neotenous readiness of the neuroplastic brain was the condition that was selected for, not an animal language. It is this that led to the acquisition of the motor-arm that enabled the voluntary naming of objects as well as their recirculation and the frontal extraction of the secondary features embedded in them. These were then used in articulations that gave us language along with the ability to match its verbal representations with the template of the spatiotemporal and causal reality of the world. It is all there: the cascade of events that gave the brain the off-line mechanism to monitor itself and to generate choice, which, as we shall see, plays a critical part in the functional autonomy that is free will in a deterministic world.

In this chapter, I have outlined the two-stage construction of language and the process by which the ability to name objects evolved into an articulated instrument. In the next chapter, before I follow its progress in the evolutionary context, I shall account for the neural device that is the key to our ability to think. In spite of its enormous significance, the device is hidden from view. This is because it is immersed in the processing tumult of the functioning brain, and current modeling requires some subtlety to discover it.

A DEVICE TO MOVE MOUNTAINS: DUAL OUTPUT, SINGLE FOCUS

Evolution is the one agency in nature that creates new phenomena.

—Jacob Bronowski, *A Sense of the Future* (1977)

At this point, I want to highlight evolution's gift to humanity. Evolution's gift to us is the power to focus, to hold the attention at will, to concentrate, reflect, and circumvent the ape brain's distractibility. It is the pathway to knowledge, to science and invention, to the understanding of the world and of the "self" itself that understands.

The way our understanding of ourselves and the world was achieved is a tour de force. Consider, then, that the living organism is one of complex interactions, a hierarchy of juggling acts. There is no stasis, no permanence in structure or function. The substrate of the human body's homeostasis is one of replenishment and rebuilding. Of the 25 trillion red blood cells in circulation, 2.5 million are destroyed and rebuilt every second. The skeleton, a seemingly stable structure, is continuously being remodeled and renewed, while all cell types have differing longevities and are replaced or, in some cases, maintained by supplementary cells that are just as transient as the rest of this incessant flux. The raw material for this immense undertaking comes from recycling and the ingestion of nutrients, a never-ending process.

The living system's quest for maintaining high-quality and continuous information processing is no less impressive. The organs of sense are geared to cope with an ever-changing environment, while the individual receptors continually flicker to ensure the flow of novel input needed to prevent habituation. Nystagmus[1] (the subliminal flicker of the eye), for example, ensures that the retinal cells are always exposed to marginally different aspects of the input. While nystagmus is good for steadiness of vision, the human brain too, if it is to prevent its attention from wandering, must find a mechanism with which it can maintain a steady focus and have time to make a considered response. In what follows, I account for how this key feature of concentrated human thought is achieved and what neural mechanisms support it.

The device I am about to outline is yet another by-product of the motor-wiring for language. The precondition of our ability to speak and think is that every referent[2] be represented by two percepts. The first is the modality percept (visual, auditory, or somatosensory); the second is its acquired companion, the word that stands for it. Their meaning is shared, and they constitute a mutually evocative associative bond. Communication, speech, and thought are, as we have seen in chapters 4 and 5, possible only when there is a word that stands for the percept. This is because only the word, the motor-wired symbol, can be uttered (thought or spoken), but never the modality percept of vision or somatosensation that we experience. So it is by courtesy of the word that the human brain is able to access its own modality experience and, through communication, the modality experience of others.

We are now coming to a point of real interest: the managing of words, whether as single entities or in the dynamic flow of language, involves a new interhemispheric transaction. The transaction modifies the brain's attentional routine in the following way. In the infrahuman context, all percepts that are focused upon constitute bilaterally symmetrical twin excitations, that is to say, identical representations of the referent. In the asymmetric human brain, the modality representation of the referent (say, the visual experience of an object) is restricted primarily to the right hemisphere. The left hemisphere's representation is now that of its symbolic substitute, the word. This is like turning identical twins into fraternal ones. The result is that the dual attentional searchlights of the arousal system, designed to focus on homotopic sites[3] in the hemispheres, have now to focus on disparate pairs, comprising modality percepts on the one hand and their word-representations on the other. To manage the synchronized handling of these sites, linked as they are by their shared referents, an accommodating attentional oscillation takes place between them. To activate it we need only utter the word that means the thing, or experience the thing (say, visually) that signifies the word. The two represent each other quite specifically and either of them elicits the other. The technicalities that underpin the oscillation are simple and will be discussed presently, but the consequences of this oscillation are of the greatest importance. They enable the brain to stay locked on to any salient item it chooses—that is to say, to concentrate and not be distracted by competing stimuli (as is the animal brain) or lose focus through habituation.

The oscillation, which is under voluntary muscle control, is a neural device that empowers the brain to apportion its attention and to hold it steady on the salience of its choice. As a result, the attention of the human brain is no longer a puppet on a string but a voluntary device it can use at will to remarkable effect. This is how it works: the attention that locks onto a given percept is switched at once to the word with which it is associated. This means that well before the referent (the percept) loses the attentional focus, its word-companion is already holding onto it. In the same manner, well before the word fades, the attention is once more back with the percept. The mutually excitatory to and fro can continue as long as the brain needs it to come up with the optimal response. So familiar is this attentional oscillation that we hardly notice it, let alone recognize the role it plays in giving us the steady focus for the mental generation of cognitive responses. Yet, if we name an object, any object, we at once begin the oscillating cycle. So as we hold our attention on the object, within seconds we are bound to notice that it is no longer the object that we are aware of but our own attending to it. However, within seconds this phase of the cycle too is replaced, and we are back with the object that started the oscillation. What the flicker of nystagmus achieves for the eye, the oscillation of the attention confers on the brain. It turns uninterrupted processing from stimulus to response into steady fixation, while in the same breath it highlights the sense of agency that the proprioception of the word-phase of the to-and-fro cycle always generates.

The neural innovation just described sheds light on how the language process generates the self-sensation that always accompanies our wakeful state. It shows how simple awareness, boosted by the brain's internal processing of itself, becomes conscious of what it is doing and that *it* is doing it.

The sustained focus on a given referent that the oscillation device makes possible alters the brain's processing

The neural innovation just described sheds light on how the language process generates the self-sensation that always accompanies our wakeful state.

routine in an important way: it prolongs the fleeting moment between input and output, allowing the brain more time to bring together and integrate disparate aspects of experience, creating a kind of global workspace.[4] These aspects would otherwise be unattainable for the generation of higher-quality responses. The animal brain, having no mechanism to hold back its instant responses, cannot generate cognitively superior behavior in this way.

Antonio Damasio (2010) describes how the human brain uses its new acquisition

> to hold extensive memory records, not only of
> motor skills but also of the facts and events …
> these depending on the ability to reconstruct and
> manipulate memory records in a working brain
> space … an off-line holding area where time can be
> suspended during a delay and decisions freed from
> the tyranny of immediate response.

Since such behavior is displayed only by the conscious human brain, the global workspace is thought to be the function of consciousness. At variance with this assumption, the model I am proposing reveals that the language mechanism is the generative source of both these aspects of mind—that is, of consciousness on the one hand and of the global workspace on the other. Consciousness (as we have seen in chapter 2) is the function of the self-feeling that language generates, while the global workspace is the extended time span that the oscillation always brings about. The co-occurrence of the two is responsible for the reasonable, though mistaken, assumption that the global workspace of the human brain is made possible by the conscious state. In fact, both aspects are neurofunctional consequences of speech and thought.

Returning to the oscillation paradigm, it is important to note that every phase of it, every turn from word to percept and percept to word, is a technically novel event and as such is supplied with fresh arousal energy by the brainstem's reticular activation system.[5] What we have here is a protective umbrella for cognition that guarantees lasting salience for the language process as a whole—that is to say, for whatever is being featured by the neural technique of attentional oscillation. This, as can be imagined, confers amazing powers on the brain. No longer is it necessary for an individual percept to be attention-binding by virtue of its own salience (as it is in the animal brain). All the attention it needs is now at its disposal because of the stable focus of the speech event in which it is participating.

On the strength of the above, I propose that the neural transactions of the oscillation form a protective frame in which word-labeled percepts can come and go, be chopped up and changed, or be taken up again as the communication in progress demands. This is nothing short of a breakthrough to open-ended cognition. It frees up the brain's word-percept repertoire for instant use "on the cheap," that is, well below the intensity threshold for attention-binding and motor-response to occur. In this privileged format, percepts can move in and out of the speech-frame, mental operations can be carried out, and conclusions arrived at need not be implemented at once, but can be stored, modified, or canceled. The format is ideal for tentative trial-and-error runs, because it is the speech frame and not the contents it features that holds the attention in oscillation.

Therefore, in light of this, it is not surprising that we feel ideational freedom to fashion, if not outright create, our intrapsychic experiences. What we have here is a remarkable combination of the oscillation device (the key to our ability to concentrate) and the privileged language frame that frees us from the burden of immediate and compulsive delivery. The oscillation empowers us to hold our concentration at will, while the language frame opens this instrument of the mind for the unlimited and unconstrained exploration of the world of which it is a part.

Attentional oscillation as a neural device for integrating hemispherically disparate inputs is not a new idea. Robert Ornstein (1972), for example, observed that "rapid switching of the attention between alternating modes of thought may be occurring," and Marcel Kinsbourne (1978) concluded that "the logic of symmetrically attending to asymmetric disparate excitations all but demands something like an oscillation paradigm." Yet, in spite of such insightful and promising remarks, oscillation could not at the time be taken up in a broader neurological context. This is not surprising. Much detailed brain mapping and localization of functions had to become available before complex interactions between them, such as attention oscillation, could be identified.

The role of the frontal lobes in using the brain's power to concentrate and hold salient percepts in focus is quite significant. For one thing, anatomically modern humanity's displacement of the large-brained but low-browed Neanderthals must have involved improved frontal functioning, and it is important to know what this functioning entailed. The answer to this question lies in the frontal lobes' special relationship with the rest of the cortex, and even more with the brainstem, the activity of which as an excitatory powerhouse the frontal lobes are able to mobilize. Importantly, it is by way of this special link that the brain's dependence on sensory sources for generating arousal can be circumvented and an auto-excitatory facility brought into play. To have a range of sensory but also self-generated salience to focus on as well as the motor facility to direct the attention any which way enables the brain to bypass the on-line response (the only response the animal is capable of) and opt for higher-quality, off-line alternatives. It is this that gives the human brain a decisive say in managing its affairs and selecting its behavioral path.

After the breakthrough to the motor-wiring of the speech areas, it took some time for the language instrument to evolve to furnish higher-quality cognitive options. Still, attentional focusing—that is, the sustained concentration on saliences by uttering the words that stood for them—was a promising start. It enabled our protohuman ancestors to lock onto percepts rather than being distracted, to perceive the world with greater clarity and to sense their active agency. These were powerful incentives to persist with the fledgling protolinguistic practice until the ancestral "Tarzan talk" evolved into articulated, syntactically sound language.

We are now in the position to take a closer look at the evolutionary and historical context out of which we have emerged as autonomous and reflectively conscious human beings.

LANGUAGE: THE TROJAN HORSE OF NEGATIVE ENTROPY

No biological phenomenon is without antecedents. The question is: how obvious are the antecedents of the human capacity for language? It is my opinion that they are not the least obvious.

—Eric H. Lenneberg, *The Biological Foundations of Language* (1967)

As we have seen, animal communication was not ancestral to language. It was the neotenous regression and the neuroplasticity of the protohuman infant that led to the rewiring of the left brain and brought into existence the precondition for an internal (off-line) way of functioning. Language is no ordinary operation. It uses a dedicated neural circuit that works almost independently of the organism's on-line response mechanism, yet it is in a position to guide and influence that response mechanism.

Composed of a rather small number of sounds or phonemes,[1] which form words (meaningful units) that can be combined in an open-ended and infinitely varied way, this digital system of language can depict in inner (mental) space all aspects of reality. It is a highly flexible system, constrained only by the demand that its output should faithfully reflect the spatiotemporal and causal characteristics of the world. As the initial naming practice of the newly motor-wired brain began to expand and the articulation of words for more complex expressions came on-line, it was this spatiotemporal template that the evolving articulations had to satisfy. Furthermore, it is this template that all the thousands of widely varying human tongues learn to reflect, thus demonstrating that syntax is not some hidden property of language but an external constraint that is universal and traceable.

Going back to the beginning, we must ask what the motor-facility for naming was able to do for our protohuman ancestors. Reconstructing those early conditions, it is feasible to assume that for some time after the breakthrough, about 150,000 years ago, protohuman awareness was not unlike that of the speech-impaired who can name but cannot connect up the items that are named. This means that early humanity's mental representation of the world was seeded with words, but large areas and aspects of experience could not be processed, spoken, or thought about. This limitation was gradually overcome and a syntax of sorts duly achieved. However, for some millennia after the breakthrough, evolution of the fully fledged language instrument was impeded by harsh physical conditions and a serious lexical bottleneck.

It is not difficult to explain the relatively long (though in evolutionary terms rather short) lead-in period between the motor-wiring of percepts and the unmistakable evidence of language-based reasoning at around 50,000 years ago. The homogeneity of the human genome and the mitochondrial identity of all members of our species point to a singular beginning, a family or small group of related individuals somewhere in southern or eastern Africa. It was a modest beginning with long doubling times of growth in a hostile world fraught with danger.

With reference to human origins and confirming the thesis that it was the motor-wiring of the speech-areas that started the ball rolling, Derek Bickerton (2009) quotes Noam Chomsky as saying:

> In some small group from which we all descend, a rewiring of the brain took place. ... The individual so rewired had many advantages: capacities for complex thought, planning, interpretation and so on. The capacity is transmitted to offspring coming to predominate. ... It is not easy to imagine an account of human evolution that does not assume at least this much, in one or another form.

Chomsky's assumption is correct, as is his conclusion (noted in chapter 3) that human language is not animal communication writ large.

During the time, perhaps tens of millennia, that followed the breakthrough from *erectus* to *sapiens*, it was this numerically insignificant but mitochondrially homogeneous group that thrived, multiplied, and spread across the Eurasian landmass. It was this group that eventually reached, by way of glacially exposed land-bridges and watercraft, the continent of Australia and the world of islands. This amazing and successful dispersion tells us that the new breed was able to overcome all obstacles, whether of distance, climate, or competing species, hominid or otherwise. It also speaks of curiosity, drive, adaptability, and significantly of the organizational and communicational skills that made it all possible, traits that bear witness to the existence of minds.

There is evidence of insightful reasoning already around the 100,000-year mark. Bickerton (2009), for example, cites the Áterian point from North Africa. This was a weapon whose manufacture involved four kinds of material: stone for the point, wood for the shaft, mastic (a sticky resin from a bush that grows around the Mediterranean), and gut or vine to bind the point to the shaft—impossible to make without off-line (mental) planning for its production. To quote Bickerton:

Tools start to shape up a little. People begin to use ochre and other pigments to decorate their bodies. ... Types of stone, used for tool manufacture, are found hundreds of miles from their sources, suggesting that some form of trade had started up. That meant contact between groups that probably didn't even speak the same proto-language.

So although there isn't a great deal of archaeological evidence of our early ancestors' abilities and achievements, the improvements in central nervous functioning are quite apparent. This indicates an awareness of agency (a sense of active self) and an effective-enough off-line mechanism able to cope with the world. So after the early millennia of dispersion of the vanishingly small population had passed and Cro-Magnon man was furnishing unmistakable evidence of cultural activity, it was really the cumulative outcome of what had been taking place all along.

At this point I want to reflect on the lexical bottleneck that constrained and limited what our ancestors were able to think, plan, and implement. Although they were in possession of a brain that was wired up for speech and were aware of themselves, as are we, they could not have had the words to reflect in depth and to do more than cope and survive. Although there can be no fossil records of early language, we can nevertheless form a fairly good idea of what it was like. Data serving as a possible template for the

At this point I want to reflect on the lexical bottleneck that con-strained and limited what our ancestors were able to think, plan, and implement.

rate and the formative conditions of language expansion can, for example, be found in K. C. Wu's book, *The Chinese Heritage* (1982):

At the turn of this present century, the "oracle bones" began to make their appearance and from 1928 on, repeated excavations have taken place at several sites. The oracle bones are so called by Western scholars because the bones were used for divination. What is important for our discussions is that from the inscriptions archeologists have learnt that the total of the written vocabulary at this period, the 14th century B.C. stands at some 3000 characters. When Xu Shen compiled his first dictionary of Chinese in the 2nd century A.D. the number of characters rose to 9353. Thus it took some 14 centuries for the vocabulary to grow three-fold. The rate of growth is about 10 percent a century, computing cumulatively. In the 18th century A.D. the Kang Xi dictionary was published containing 42,174 entries. Taking Xu Shen's dictionary as a base, it took therefore some 16 centuries to grow more than fourfold and interestingly enough the rate of growth is again a cumulative 10 percent for every century. So let us use this formula and compute backwards, starting from the 14th century B.C. when the Shang vocabulary is understood to have reached 3000. For the 15th century B.C. we should have 2700, for the 16th century B.C. 2430 and so on. By the time we arrive at the 27th century, we should find that the number of characters stands at 766. Admittedly this is approximation at its broadest and crudest, nevertheless to anyone who is familiar with the requirements of so called "basic English," the significance of this approximation must be inescapable. For it is generally conceded that if one knows some 800 words, one can go about one's daily business without much trouble. If this is the case then we have approximated the time the Chinese had the use of 800 characters precisely at the time of the Yellow Emperor.

What is significant here is that it was the so-called Yellow Emperor who is taken to have united the Chinese provinces, put an end to the nomadic way of life, and turned the population to agriculture and living in permanent settlements. The complex communicational demands of the new practices, relations, artifacts, and circumstances created the need for additional linguistic tools to cope with the changing situation. K. C. Wu's data highlight the link between demand and supply, circumstance and language response to meet it. It identifies the reasons for the linguistic "take-off" when, after the Ice Age and the Stone Age, a major shift in lifestyle occurred that called for more accurate communication, including the eventual keeping of (written) records. Allowing for local variations, then, this can be seen as the template for language expansion and fine-tuning of the means of communication in all the so-called cradles of civilization.

Projecting the regression-line further back in time and assuming that the ways of the hunter-gatherer or of the nomadic herdsman would change little over centuries, or even millennia, we come to a plateau of an essential and basic core vocabulary of a few hundred indispensable words. Limited as such a protolexicon may have been, it had to be enough to achieve a syntax of sorts with gestural assistance as well as to support a sense of "self" and provide moderate control of on-line behavior. While early *sapiens* could not have had the sophistication and the lexical depth for serious reflection, they were well across the line; it was only a question of time, changing circumstances, and expanding vocabulary for their mental representation of the world to be perfected and the syntactic accuracy needed for it fully achieved.

The enriched, stabilized, and articulated language instrument is awesome. The accurate representation of the world was, however, only its initial accomplishment. Repeated reflections on the template of reality were to lead in time to the revision of the template itself, to questions about matter and its substrate. It was language that empowered the human brain to seek a rational understanding of the world and to go beyond mythology.

More difficult than the decoding of the ins and outs of the material world is the modeling of the conscious mind that does the decoding. The laws of physics it knows to be governing the world seem not quite to apply to itself, so it is perplexed. The apparently irresolvable contradiction between determinism and the experience of free will is the core of the problem, and our task here is to clarify it.

Before I come to humanity's "functional autonomy" in chapter 10, though, we need to look at a few important issues. Foremost is the mind. In the next chapter, I examine the term, specify its neural structure, and then identify the brain-module that underpins it and the language-function that is the key to communication, reflection, and thought.

WHAT IS THIS THING
CALLED MIND?

The entity we call mind is perhaps that part of the brain's functional organization of which we are conscious.

—Noam Chomsky, *Language and Mind* (1968)

We speak of the mind as if we know what it is, but we have only the vaguest of ideas of its true nature. To think of it merely as the functioning of the brain is just as misguided as to take it to be a nonmaterial entity. In this chapter, I show that what we are talking about is a distinct and robust neural system, a system that was born when the brain gained access to itself. There is no justification for the confusion that surrounds the term "mind."

Not that the imprecision is in any way surprising. Its semantic roots reach back to antiquity, when guesswork was all we had to go on. Even today we face time-honored traditions, folk-psychological as well as religious, and ridding the mind of this legacy is bound to be an uphill struggle. Nor is brain science itself innocent of misusing the term. Take, for example, David Oakley's (1985) claim that "the emergence of neural modeling corresponds to the emergence of mind"—a wild generalization, for, if all neural representations, from the simple sensory alertness of the paramecium to our reflective consciousness, are regarded as instances of mind, the term loses all specificity and is rendered useless.

The mind is an exclusively human neural system, first instantiated when, empowered by the motor-wiring of the speech-areas, the brain gained access to itself—or, to be quite precise, when it gained access to those aspects of itself that the off-line mechanism of language was able to reach. This is clearly a good deal less than the total range of our brain's functioning. Therefore, to equate the total range of our brain's functioning with the mind, that is, a subsystem of the brain that has only limited access to it, is quite wrong. By contrast, what is quite right is that with language the brain can access its reservoir of percepts and solve problems that are beyond the reach of the organism's on-line response capability. This new function is not possessed by the animal brain. It is created and maintained by the human brain's off-line operation. It results in a world of self-generated experience that is always accompanied by a sensation of an active "self" that is part of the experience. Hence, what the mind generates is inseparable from the generating mind. Though the subjective experience of this is inaccessible to introspection, its technicalities are easy to trace.

I am writing this and you are reading it by the courtesy of our minds, the neural system over which we have voluntary muscle control. Functioning freely within its operational range and without the constraints of on-line consequences, the mind is the source of the robust category that is called imagination. It is this product of the mind that generates all the innovation, invention, science, and insight whose results, when connected with the organism's quest for success and survival, constitute an evolutionary device of enormous significance. Affirming the value of imagination, our language-managed (mental) sphere of operations, John Maynard Smith and Eörs Szathmary (2009) remind us that

> one important aspect of language is that we can talk about things we could never do. To perform complex meaningful actions we must go through many impractical ones in our head. To do good, solid science, we need well-developed fantasy and imagination.

Let us now take a closer look at the source of our imagination, which is, of course, the mind. Significantly, the mind is the only neural system that generates self-reflection, that is to say, the experience of having an experience and of managing it. Recall from chapters 2 and 6 that the motor response of speech and thought generates a sensation of an active self. This sensation is part of the attentional oscillation that enables the system to reflect on what it wants, and it includes its own reflection on the reflecting self. No other neuronal system can do this; the animal brain, lacking the off-line mechanism for the task, that is, language, can never rise above the level of unreflective, purely sensory awareness of its world.

Benjamin Libet's (1990) "time-on" theory corroborates the role of self-reflection in the mind. Neural events are time-dependent, so that it takes longer to achieve higher levels of integration. Thus, neural transactions of less than 300 to 350 milliseconds (the level needed for awareness) take place automatically, in neural darkness, so to speak. Once the level of awareness is reached, the integrated sensory data (making up the endogram) are evaluated by the brainstem, and an on-line response must follow—on-line because the animal brain has no other mechanism with which to respond. By contrast, the mind-endowed human brain has the off-line mechanism of speech or thought with which to abort, modify, replace, and control the would-be action impulse, or, if on reflection it seems suitable, to let it through to the motor system for its on-line implementation. (See chapter 10 for the evaluation of this mechanism in the framework of the organism's functional autonomy.) Libet's time-on theory is, therefore, a three-tiered arrangement of "subawareness" (working in neural darkness), "awareness" (the level of the animal brain with on-line responding), and "reflective, human awareness" (characterized by off-line internal processing and conscious self-management). Importantly, the third tier (the tier of the mind) is built on extra structures, functions, and adaptations for managing the endogram from within and for reentering the reflective process as experience. Human awareness normally uses the two top tiers, shifting in and out of the reflective tier as required, idling in the middle tier and falling to the bottom tier during sleep and reduced blood and oxygen supply. The top tier, the mind, is therefore a physical process and not some structureless, ephemeral abstraction, as naïve experience often suggests. In any event, the operational freedom that this neuronal system—the mind—confers on the brain is the passport to a world where it is an active player in the shaping of outcomes.

Confirming the reality and role of this neural system we call mind, Hassler (1978) noted that

> we must therefore conclude that our actual conscious
> experience embraces only a small area of all that
> can be potentially brought to awareness. The field
> of awareness is restricted and excludes a number of
> engrams. This leads us to postulate the existence of
> neuronal systems that are independent of most other

neuronal systems and that have the ability to activate at a given moment only a small fraction of the huge mass of potentially retrievable material stored in the integrative cortical areas that are not primary sensory fields.

The mind's relationship to the rest of the brain is of genuine interest. If we can be conscious only of what is just now in focus, we can use the condition of entry into this focus to gain insight into the mind's jurisdiction, demarcation, and role in relation to the other subsystems of the brain. It is, for example, feasible to consider the blocking of the entry of a given input (its suppression or repression) as a response to threatening content. However, for the brain to decide what is threatening content and what is not, an initial entry into the brain on the unconscious plane is necessary. As the processing of incoming stimuli is a time-dependent affair during which percepts evolve gradually, inhibitory innervations can come into play and prevent their full integration and entry into the focus of awareness.

Tachistoscopic[1] (high-speed) visual presentation of emotionally threatening material confirms that such an initially unconscious entry always takes place and that it is the subliminal response to the rising (i.e., early) phase of the percept that leads to its facilitation or its suppression. This draws the attention to a censoring mechanism that operates in conjunction with the neuronal system of the mind. Should it turn out that the censoring function is not under the jurisdiction of the mind, then we need to know how it works and how it relates to the mind it is designed to protect.

To answer these questions, we must turn to the inhibitory mechanisms that are at work between higher and lower centers of integration in the central nervous system. Their task is to maintain an advantageous balance between interacting subsystems in the intuitively sensed interest of the organism. Higher centers can override lower ones, though the lower too are able to veto the higher centers where issues of survival are involved. Confirming this, Gerald Edelman (1992) noted that "such a view of attention still concedes the major overriding significance to non-conscious mechanisms and to the orienting behavior, mediated by global mapping in response to emergencies." On the strength of this, it is quite conceivable that the suppression of subliminally sensed material is not the doing of the mind.

In his *Logic of the Living Brain*, Gerd Sommerhoff (1974) traces the pathways of a given neural input. His findings are particularly relevant for the clarification of the mechanisms of suppression. To paraphrase his results:

An ultrarapid stream of excitations sweeps from the representational cortices to the frontal evaluation cortex. From here it descends to the limbic area and the reticular formation, where it is given or denied further facilitation by the arousal mechanism. The decision for or against facilitation depends on the emotional implications of the input. If accepted by this subcortical censoring gate, the stream is sent once more to the representational and evaluative centers of the cortex, but this time with the attention/arousal component added to lead to awareness or motor-response or both. If the input is not accepted by the censor, all further arousal is denied by way of inhibitory innervations and the sequence is terminated without reentry into higher areas of consciousness.

Sommerhoff's analysis makes it clear that the mind operates, or more precisely is permitted to operate, only under the control of the other subsystems of the brain. Unaware of the protective measures that surround it, the conscious mind is in no position to realize that it is being monitored and guided. Its information about itself is, in fact, so limited that it can entertain and rationalize quite fanciful ideas without fear of contradiction. Its self-validation is solipsistic; it uses its impression of itself to prove its self-impression, and this allows it to believe it has entelechy-like[2] free will or is the "ghost in the machine," or both.

Whatever self-characterization the conscious brain manages to come up with (its introspective roots will be

Unaware of the protective measures that surround it, the conscious mind is in no position to realize that it is being monitored and guided.

explored in the next chapter), it needs sophisticated equipment for the job. The equipment is language, the system's motor-arm and means of delivery. Its evolution has been covered in chapters 4, 5, and 7. Here we look at the emergent, uniquely human brain module that underpins its functioning. It is a complex and topographically distributed system that involves a variety of special adaptations, supplementary neural growth, and functional arrangements. The toolkit for generating statements must have:

- Building blocks: word-percepts as units of transactions

- Work-routines (grammar) to organize the material to meet the specifications of syntax

- A memory-bank (long- as well as short-term) with a retrieval mechanism

- A percept- and concept-generating capacity to furnish the mind with what is needed for comprehension and coping

To satisfy the list of requirements, the working mind draws on and integrates the following structures:

- The speech-areas

- The frontal lobes to oversee and focus on the output

- The cross-hemispheric link (the corpus callosum) for integrating the denotative and connotative aspects of the output

- The supramodal association areas[3] to generate percepts, concepts, and schemas for the use of language

- The brainstem arousal system to give high-energy priority to speech-thought production

- The extensive collateral arborization[4] of neurons that rewires the human brain and boosts the language instrument with supplementary connections and additional growth

It is important to realize that the arborization just mentioned is mind-induced and confirms that the brain subsystem that underpins it makes use of specially generated nerve tissue, over and above the modifications, adaptations, and recombinations of preexisting structures. It is also clear that without this multifaceted subsystem the brain could not manage and mold its ongoing experience and reflect on what it is doing. It could not be aware of itself as an active agent, as it would be fully immersed in the on-line response procedures of old. Without a mind to reflect on itself and to make changes, if necessary, we would be like our cousins the great apes: subtle and intuitive but not under the brain's deliberate and insightful control.

Nor would we have the mental world we now possess, the knowledge and the choice we generate for managing our behavioral path.

As we have seen, the off-line (language) response can cut in and change the course of events at the 400–450 millisecond level of neural integration, where, if an off-line system did not exist, an online motor-response would have to occur. This new dispensation gives the brain an active role in the decision-making process by generating mental options for the brainstem to consider. Although, as we shall see in chapter 10, this self-generated choice does not amount to free will, it is an important component of the functional autonomy that language-based reflective consciousness has given us. The way this breakthrough has come about, or even that a breakthrough to insightful data processing has in fact taken place, is more than the naïve mind is able to comprehend. Hence, it is free to think what it wants: the "agent within," the creation myth it likes, or the mystery that defies the mind. E. O. Wilson (1978) captured the naïve mind's predicament in an imaginative and evocative way:

> An uneasy stalemate exists, leaving the towering psychological enigma of self-consciousness hanging perilously between the murky swamps of metaphysics and the lush but uninhabitable pastures of introspective analysis. Trapped, like some lost

soul in this awful limbo, it admits of no scientific explanation.

Yet, as we have seen, there is no "towering psychological enigma" or "limbo," and the whole shebang can be well accounted for. In other words, the qualitative changes that made the brain an active player in generating and managing its experience can be modeled with clarity. To leave the accounting of the human experience to the guesswork of the naïve mind is, therefore, not an acceptable option. To show what it can lead to, in the next chapter I shall detail the illusions and the misconstructions that the naïve mind's introspection cannot help but deliver.

THE ALCHEMY OF
SELF-DECEPTION:
INTROSPECTION AT WORK

If physicalism is to be defended, the phenomenological
features of experience must themselves be given a
physical account.
—Thomas Nagel, "Physicalism" (1965)

I now turn to examine what the conscious mind, when
left to its own resources, is bound to make of itself. I show
how introspection is constrained to generate the impression that we are entelechy-like, free-willing entities. To do
this I identify four seemingly unassailably solid sources of
internal evidence. The self-deception that will be demon-
strated shows us with clarity what can happen if Konrad
Lorenz's (1978) insightful warning is not heeded:

At an early age I realised that in the interest
of objectivity a scientist must understand the

physiological and psychological mechanisms by which experiences are conveyed to man. He must understand them and for the same reason why a biologist must know his microscope and understand its optical functions. Namely, in order to avoid taking for one of the characteristics of the object he is observing, something that in fact results from the limitations of his instrument.

The first piece of apparently solid evidence is that the conscious mind *knows* (by default, as will be shown) that it is free because it cannot know itself as unfree, that is, caused or determined. This is because the conscious state, the condition in which the brain is able to reflect and think, "switches on" at a definite point along the neurofunctional event sequence whose earlier components (those occurring before the onset of the reflectively conscious state) are always inaccessible and, therefore, unknowable. This is in line with Libet's "time-on" theory with respect to event components that are too short in duration to reach the integration threshold for awareness at the 300–350 millisecond level. Since self-accessibility is thought dependent and thinking is an off-line response that gets switched on, there can be no memory of what there was before it occurred. It is as if we were to ask what a lamp had been illuminating before it was turned on. The question of "what went before" is, therefore, technically as well as experientially meaningless. The reflectively aware brain can have no memory of what has brought it on, because when that event was about to take place it did not yet exist. The conscious state is always restricted to the experience that is just then occurring. Even remembered material is only input in the present. On the strength of these natural impressions, the mind-equipped brain is, therefore, in no position to question its direct experience, which is that

it has no identifiable causal source;

it came about in some indefinable way; and

it is an entelechy-like entity in a physical frame.

The second piece of supposedly solid evidence is the conscious mind's *feeling* that it is the source of its own self-experience. This impression stems from the proprioception, the active "doing-sensation" that always accompanies what we speak or think. The result is that we cannot doubt the authorship of what we experience and must perforce conclude that our self-experience too is in fact our own production. On the strength of introspection, and strange as it may seem, we cannot help but feel that our self-experience is self-caused and that the entelechy-like impression of our identity is correct.

The third piece of supposed evidence is our sense of volitional freedom.[1] To show how it works, a brief digression is called for. Importantly, the animal brain's on-line responses are always congruent with brainstem values, deeply sensed biobehavioral determinants. For the animal, the question of brain-generated choice cannot arise, as there is no "off-line" mechanism to create it.

By contrast, the human brain's generative facility brings a new element into the picture. This has to do with the two supplementary motor areas on the superior surfaces of the two hemispheres, the structures that register pre-action potentials, whether the cortices are human or animal. However, whereas the animal brain's pre-action potentials are fully dependent on the concrete situation, the human brain is able to generate pre-action potentials just by thinking about possible actions. This involves the induction of the off-line mechanism to produce hypothetical alternatives that can be evaluated by the brainstem and implemented to complete the sequence. This implies a range of thought-created options to assist the decision-making process in the selection of an appropriate and optimal response. It is this facility that enables the conscious mind to transcend the concrete constraints of the non-mind-equipped and unreflective brain of the ape.

Yet, in spite of the human brain's remarkable breakthrough into thought-guided cognition, introspection remains a force to reckon with. When it comes to self-understanding, it leads us astray in a new way: unlike our infrahuman cousins, we *can* say to ourselves that we *could*

Unlike our infrahuman cousins, we *can* say to ourselves that we *could* do this or that, because we have language to say it with and mental alternatives to say it about.

do this or that, because we have language to say it with and mental alternatives to say it about. Furthermore, we *can* think about how we *could* implement other options, and this gives us the sensation and the compelling data so that we have latitude for self-guidance and have freedom to choose alternatives. Hence, we are convinced that we *will* our actions and that what we opt for is the outcome of a process that is different in kind from what is taking place on the infrahuman plane.

Now, while these impressions are right in indicating that a momentous change has occurred, they are wrong about the nature of the change. The new processing routine *does not* bypass deterministic causation in absolute terms; it only modifies the standard framework of the stimulus-to-response transition. It does this by inserting mental alternatives into the "ham phase" of the input–output "sandwich." This furnishes the brainstem with self-generated material and will be shown to be a critical aspect of the brain's functional autonomy (chapter 10); but it is not an entelechy-type of volitionality. Yet this is precisely what is being insisted on by those who feel that whatever we choose, we could have chosen otherwise—in other words, that we have free will and are in charge.

The argument that supports this claim is compelling but unsound. It hinges on the unverifiable assumption that we could have opted for what we did not. This leads to the circularity that if we had, after all, opted for what we did not in fact opt for, what was until then hypothetical proof would in its turn need to be similarly proven. However, this "proof" too would be in need of an imagined alternative that would have to remain unactualized. The conclusion is clear. The entelechy-type of free will—the impression of the introspecting mind—is a chimera, and the insinuation of itself into the decision-making process is a mere rationalization. The explanation of the human brain's functional autonomy, the source of the mind's misconstructions, lies in a combination of cortical and subcortical processes: in a process that is only half-accessible to the introspecting mind.

The fourth piece of supposed evidence is the mind-equipped brain's sensing that there is something intangible and mysterious about it, something that defies concrete analysis and cannot be captured by language or thought. The source of this impression is that the self as percept—the entity that is thinkable—can only be post hoc to the self-feeling that the utterance proprioceptively engenders. Note that the self, when thought or spoken of, is not quite the same as the feeling of it. The discrepancy between the two is clear enough indication that thinking, the sole instrumentality for rational analysis, is not able to fully capture our experience of the self. This is because by the time the self-feeling becomes thinkable, it has undergone its transformation into the percept form and is no longer the experience it was, only its representation. In short, what we are able to think about is the percept-entity into which the self-feeling is translated, but not the self-feeling itself. The very process that creates thinking, that is, the "off-line" mechanism, is then responsible for generating the proprioception, the source of the self-feeling that cannot be thought of at the time of its occurrence. From this it follows that the self must always seem in some way elusive to itself and that thinking about it only deepens this impression. A sense of mystery, therefore, lingers as a permanent, even if only a faint, side effect of our brain's functioning.

Another indication that introspection is not the way to gain insight into how our mind works is John O'Keefe's (1985) incorrect observation:

> The strangest source of the mindedness of my consciousness is the phenomenon of self-awareness, the awareness of being aware. This quasi-mystical notion, with its constant threat of tumbling the introspector into the chasm of infinitely nested awarenesses ("I am aware, that I am aware, that I am aware"), has seemed the least likely of all attributes of consciousness to admit a scientific explanation.

O'Keefe is wrong here; what seems to him to be a quasi-mystical notion ("I am aware, that I am aware, that I am aware") is in fact the technically correct depiction of the reflective mind's oscillation between what it thinks and the accompanying sensation of thinking it. The effect, though beyond the reach of introspection, is in no way mysterious. The self, when thinking about itself, enters itself into the experience of the moment both as percept and as proprioception. This results in the loss of contrast between what is thought and who thinks it. Trying to sort it out with introspection makes it worse because of the extra proprioception that the exercise generates. Without a model to shed light on the subtle technicalities involved, introspection deepens the mystery and falls into the trap of mind–body dualism, where common sense no longer reigns.

Then there is language, the off-line mechanism's motor-arm. It, too, generates effects that are beyond the reach of introspection. Take, for example, the reversal of the causal order when an internal (language) response to an external stimulus becomes the internal (mental) stimulus for an external (on-line) response. The conscious mind, unaware of the intervening language loop, the cause of the reversal, but aware of the conscious thought that precedes the response, is forced to conclude that *it* is the initiator, and so the entelechy is once more confirmed. In the next chapter, this seeming reversal of the causal order in the wake of the language response will be shown to play a part in the controversy over free will, muddying the waters and masking the right solution.

On the strength of the mind's naïve impression, we can conclude that introspection is the generative source of delusional self-characterizations. Furthermore, without insight into how this comes about, the mind has no choice but to accept the "self" as an autonomous, uncaused causal agent, an agent that has a causal effect on an otherwise deterministic world, quite freely and of its own accord. It is also significant that a more or less typecast image of this inner entity keeps emerging with just about unfailing consistency and regardless of culture, context, societal sophistication, primitiveness, modernity, or anything else.

This is how Nicholas Humphrey (1984) puts it:

Thus, when allowance is made for certain eccentricities there is a remarkable convergence in the accounts which people of all races and all cultures give of what reflexive consciousness reveals to them. The gist of it—and I am attempting here to summarize, not to caricature—is this: In association with my body there exists a spirit, conscious of its existence and continuity in time. This is the spirit, mind, soul, which I call "I." Among the chief attributes which I possess are these: I can act, I can perceive, I can feel. Thus it is I, who, by exertion of my will, brings about almost all my significant bodily actions, etc.

The predictable nigh-universality of self-experience strongly suggests that almost uniform conditions surround its genesis. It is plausible that the elements that shape the self are wired in at an early age with the young child's rapidly expanding representational schemas. This is likely because the self-experience of the mind supplies itself quite automatically with the confirmatory evidence that the entelechy-like self-characterization requires. This goes on as a matter of course and with a sense of irrefutable factuality that makes for faithlike certitude, so that no reasonable doubt as to the truth of the matter can arise. In short, the young child grows up with, as well as grows into, a core perception of him- or herself and the entity within. Furthermore, nothing during the child's formative years can convince it that his or her self-impressions are operational side effects without ontological reality of any kind. Thus the child is predisposed to think of him- or herself in terms of soul-, spirit-, and agent-like internal representations and is programmed to resist technically more sophisticated models of his or her inner workings. The unavoidable conclusion is that the naïve mind is the unwitting author of a self-characterization that is binding and intuitively persuasive, yet loaded with false ontological implications.

We have looked at the work of introspection and what the unaided mind is likely to make of itself. Yet language, the source of these products, need not be a cognitive trap but can become a liberating passport to ever-deepening insights into the nature of the world and of the conscious mind itself. The continual development of science and the increasing sophistication of technology bear witness to an internal process of revision, a reworking of the contents of the brain that renders accessible what used to be beyond conceivability. What remains for us to investigate is the way the evolutionary process has managed to raise the human organism, immersed as it is in a deterministic world, to a level where it operates and feels itself to be operating as a functionally autonomous, causal codeterminant of outcomes. This is the problem I explore in the next chapter.

FUNCTIONAL AUTONOMY: THE TRIUMPH OF EVOLUTIONARY BOOTSTRAPPING

There is free will and we have no choice about it.

—Isaac B. Singer, *In My Father's Court* (1991)

Having identified the intracortical mechanism that puts the brain in charge of itself by making its awareness reflective, we must now tackle the problem of free will, the Gordian knot at the crossroads of science and philosophy.

In an orderly world, where everything is lawfully anteceded, there is no room for autonomous sources of causation. To claim otherwise is scientific heresy and a philosophical death wish. The entelechy, the uncaused causal agent, is fiction, and, as was shown in the previous chapter on introspection, its source is delusional.

But what if it were possible to demonstrate that the breakthrough to self-accessibility and self-generated choice has led to a bootstrapping arrangement that gets around all the objections by way of a subtle selection mechanism, a mechanism that puts the brain in charge without coming into conflict with the constraints of determinism? Recall from chapter 2 that the onset of life has divided the causal chain and that the organic (living) branch has been interacting with and modifying the biosphere ever since. At first, this activity was only biochemical, but after the first phase-transition to multicellular organisms with awareness and motor leverage, it became physical as well. Finally, in the wake of the second-phase transition that led to language and reflective capability, information and knowledge were brought into play to shape the material world and free the brain to define its own course. The task is to show that this expanded causal role of the conscious human organism is brought on by traceable functional changes and that its resulting autonomy is legitimate.

To do this, we look at the mind-equipped brain's internal arrangements, in this case in combination with subcortical centers. Failure to perceive that there is such an ingenious mechanism leaves us at sea and facing the tantalizing contradiction between our apparent free will and its manifest impossibility.

Although complicated, there is a way to approach the problem. We do know that the brain's "off-line" mechanism (language) works with voluntary muscles and (as we have seen in the last chapter) can substitute its own mind-generated responses for on-line, behavioral ones. Now we need to see whether this choice-generating mechanism might be linked up with subcortical centers of decision making to form an emergent system in which the brain's mentally generated options could be the subjects of selection and, hence, be codeterminants of outcomes. While these outcomes would represent the brain's mental contribution, they would not involve an act of choosing and stepping outside the frame of determinism. In what follows, I show that such a dispensation, though unrecognized, is actually at work and constitutes the "functional autonomy" we think of mistakenly (though not without some justification) as our free will.

To begin this inquiry I go directly to Benjamin Libet's seminal experiments of 1978. Unlike the mostly abstract arguments that deal with the mind, Libet looks at the "equipment," the living brain, to gain insight into how it works and what conclusions about it are warranted. What he found was that the initiation and the preparatory phase of an act, as measured by its readiness potential in the brain, takes place before we are aware of willing or wanting it. In fact, some 300–350 milliseconds are needed to reach point "W," the point defined by Libet as the one where we become aware of willing or wanting it. This is, of course, proof positive that we never initiate an act or are its bona fide conscious source.

This may seem to be the end of the free-will story, but there is more: Libet's findings also reveal that after reaching point "W," some 150–200 milliseconds have to elapse before the motor system is given the command to proceed with its execution. This, Libet (1978) points out, gives us a window of opportunity to abort the impending act, whether by inhibiting it or by switching to another preliminary action-impulse waiting in the wings. Libet regards this as an effective "veto-function," a mechanism of interference with the impending action's implementation, and notes that "the potentiality for a form of free choice in the classical sense is not excluded by the theory, though apparently in the form of control rather than in the initiation of an act."

While Libet's 200-millisecond window of opportunity for the mind-equipped brain to veto an act and make a substitution confirms the efficacy of the "off-line" mechanism, it is not free will in any meaningful sense. This is because the decision to abort or to switch is under the same constraint of determinism as is the act to be interfered with. Furthermore, the said decision's initiation and preparatory phase, too, has to run the normal course so that our wanting to abort it is just as much the midstream realization of an act that is already in progress. To put it another way, to decide to cancel an act is as determined as is the act to be canceled, or, as Galen Strawson (1994) has noted: "Even if one has time to override one's unconscious urges, there is no free will at work if one's conscious decisions are themselves determined."

In spite of these negative conclusions about Libet's unworkable model of free will, his 200-millisecond window of opportunity turns out to be one of the vital ingredients of the functional autonomy of the human brain. This is because it is in that 200-millisecond interval that the brainstem/limbic value categories, in charge of choosing the salience to respond to, are presented with the mentally generated options and Darwinian selection comes into play. In that interval, the domain that represents the mentally generated options is exposed to the second domain, that of the criteria on the basis of which the selection of the most favored option takes place. So although Libet identified the all-important off-line component of autonomous human functioning, he failed to realize that this component, in combination with the brainstem/limbic decision-making function, does constitute a causally unimpeachable self-guidance mechanism.

This latest of the Darwinian selection mechanisms, placing the brain's mentally generated action-alternatives in the path of our subconscious decision making, works as follows. The 200-millisecond window of opportunity between Libet's "W," the onset of awareness and the triggering of an act, is enough time to sense (emotively assess) the significance of its likely outcome. We get a "gut feeling," call it intuition, of whether to proceed or not. At this point the basal ganglia, in charge of inhibition and disinhibition, come into play. They respond in terms of the sensed congruence between the impending action's expected outcome (now and for the first time available to the reflective mind) and the organism's best interest as perceived by its brainstem/limbic value-categories. To quote Gerald Edelman (1992):

> In accordance with the given plan, the basal ganglia selectively disinhibit the thalamic nuclei projecting into the cortex. This leads to the anticipatory and selective arousal of cortical areas corresponding to the motor program.

The result of this Darwinian selection process is that all the competing action impulses present at the time remain inhibited, except the one that is "felt" by the brainstem to be the most congruent with the organism's values. The conscious mind, unaware of the evaluating transaction of the brainstem that disinhibits one of the options, but aware of having thought of the option, rationalizes that *it* has done the deciding.

The mind-equipped brain's impression that it initiates, wills, and decides is, therefore, the traceable misconstruction of the thinking machine that has only half the data to go on: the action alternatives it itself is generating. The other half, the brainstem's decision making, is inaccessible and therefore unknown to it. Aware of the options it is generating and that one of these is always implemented, the mind concludes that it is all its own doing. Without evidence to the contrary and insight into the brainstem's decisive role, the misconstruction remains unchallenged, and the mind presumes that it has an entelechy-type of freedom.

The irony is that brain evolution *has* achieved the functional autonomy that feels like free will, even if the way this works cannot be known by the introspecting mind. This brings me back to the brainstem, the silent half of the free-will equation, which, in partnership with mind-generated options, forms a Darwinian selection mechanism. Neither of the two domains is problematic in any way. The first contains the mentally generated options from which the brainstem makes its selection. The options are entertained mentally and whether we create them in situ or summon them from memory, they are always to hand. Take, for example, the moment when we leave a building. We can go left or right, go back or cross the street, go home or wander about, have a snack at the sandwich bar, and all the possible permutations that can arise. We live in a rich field of options, one we keep continuously generating, though importantly not willing or initiating, and out of which our brainstem/limbic values, our "gut feeling," selects for us what is relevant in that moment. Brain-imaging techniques confirm this internal genesis, this language-induced world of options, where every instance is a fork in the road.

The irony is that brain evolution *has* achieved the functional autonomy that feels like free will, even if the way this works cannot be known by the introspecting mind.

Whereas the first domain that generates the options is mind dependent and as recent as the breakthrough to *Homo sapiens* and motor-wiring for speech, the second domain, the brainstem mechanism that does the selection, has been the decisive component of vertebrate functioning since even before reptilian times. To quote Antonio Damasio (2010), the brainstem "is the neural home of biological value, and biological value has a pervasive influence throughout the brain, in terms of structure and operations." Without biological values for guidance and response-selection, the organism would not know how or what to respond to and so how to survive. It is the brainstem that gives the green light to the motor systems of all creatures to perform on-line responses congruent with its values.

In the case of the infrahuman brain with no mentally generated options to complicate matters, the green light of disinhibition is given to the dominant salience of the moment. Decision making by the brainstem is smooth and uncomplicated. In the case of the human brain, a new situation arises. The ability to generate and to present the brainstem with a number of significant and competing saliences at the same time complicates its decision making. This can lead to stress, to hesitation and neurosis. The mechanism of selection is the same as before, but the balance between the cortex[1] and the brainstem is changed. In particular, the conscious mind, able to monitor the course of the events in which it is enmeshed, is induced to generate options congruent with the interests of the organism and therefore tempting for the brainstem to accept. This in turn highlights the functional nexus between the cortex (furnishing the first domain) and the brainstem (constituting the second), about which Damasio (2010) has this to say:

> Because of its mastery in the role of life regulator, the brain stem has long been the recipient and local processor of the information needed to represent the body and control its life. ... The brainstem continues to carry out these same functions in humans today. On the other hand, the greater complexity of the cerebral cortex has enabled detailed image-making, expanded memory capacity, imagination, reasoning, and eventually language. Now comes the big problem: notwithstanding the anatomical and functional expansion of the cerebral cortex, the functions of the brain stem were *not* duplicated in the cortical structures. The consequence of this economic division of roles is a fatal and complete interdependence of brain stem and cortex. They are *forced* to cooperate with each other.
>
> Brain evolution was faced with a major anatomo-functional bottleneck, but natural selection predictably solved it. Given that the brain stem was

still being asked to guarantee the full scope of life regulation *and* the foundations of consciousness for the entire nervous system, a way had to be found of ensuring that the brain stem influenced the cerebral cortex *and*, just as important, that the activities of the cerebral cortex influenced the brain stem. This is all the more important when we think that most external objects exist as images only in the cerebral cortex and cannot be fully imaged in the brain stem.

The interdependence of cortex and brainstem is clear but not new. What *is* new is the option-generating role of the cortex. It floods the brainstem's decision making, which, though still determined by biological values, now has to respond to material that is mind generated and is an expression of the person's disposition, interest, and character.

Regarding this causal role of the mind, it must be stressed that the knowledge, the insight, the imagination, and all the subtleties the human brain is able to introduce into its processing represent painstakingly built, accumulated, and stored information. Informational wealth, lawfully acquired, is carried and judiciously reintroduced into the causal chain to subserve a practical end. It is like the release of long-withheld potential energy to do the work that is required.

The model I am proposing shows how mentally generated, ego-congruent material enters the decision-making process and confers functional autonomy on the brain. It shows how the Darwinian mechanism of response selection, using a range of options that are run past the brainstem, though neither initiated nor willed, puts an end to the perennial free-will versus determinism debate, a debate that is anchored in the incomplete understanding of how the system works. For to say that we are entelechy-like free agents is as far off the mark as to insist that we are no more than inert links in the unbroken chain of causation. The former flies in the face of science and underwrites dualism; the latter turns the evidence of self-experience into a depressing and counterfactual farce. What I am proposing cuts the Gordian knot. It accounts for evolution's ingenious way of bootstrapping the cognitive apparatus of *Homo sapiens* into an effective causal role where, to quote Erwin Schrödinger (1967), "it can stand entropy on its head." Able to generate and to draw on sophisticated information and with physical leverage for implementation, the mind-equipped brain is now the causal codeterminant of outcomes.

In summary, the human chapter of evolution began with the neotenous regression to year one as the critical age for language. The motor-wiring of the speech areas followed, giving the brain access to itself. This led to language, to the brain's genesis of and control of saliences. This raised cognition to a higher plane and established the "self" as an integral part of its own cognition. Finally, the mind's generation of mental options, in combination with the brainstem's decision-making role, gave us the selection mechanism, the key to our functional autonomy, the only kind of freedom that can be had in a deterministic world. It is an amazing trajectory on all counts. It is the key to the limitless horizons of the mind. Reflecting on it, Stephen J. Gould (1977) had this to say:

> The evolution of consciousness can scarcely be matched as a momentous event in the history of life. There may be nothing new under the sun, but permutations of the old within complex systems can do wonders.

There is, however, another possible take on this thesis. It is I. B. Singer's whimsical conclusion, which is the epigram of this chapter: "There is free will and we have no choice about it."

ABOUT THE SELF:
FICTION AND FACT

Stranger to the Duke of Wellington: "Mr. Smith, I believe?"
Duke to the stranger: "Sir, if you can believe that, you can believe anything."

—Unknown

The model I am proposing is a single perspective whose aspects interlock and confirm one another. Without this model, the identification and clarification of consciousness, mind, the breakthrough to language, the source of syntax, free will, and the experience of the self would not be possible.

I have accounted for consciousness and matters relating to it in chapter 2, sharing Gerald Edelman's (1992) view that "there can be no science of human beings until consciousness is explained in biological terms." I have identified the mind and the brain module supporting it in chapter 8, traced the breakthrough to *Homo sapiens* to neoteny, outlined the evolution of language, and linked syntax to the context of reality in chapters 4, 5, and 7. Finally, I have shown that our experience of free will is brought on by the awareness of the role we play in the interaction of mind and brainstem, the source of decision making, in the preceding chapter. It is now time to take a closer look at the self and matters relating to it.

Rather than an arbitrary social construct or, at the other end of the spectrum, a nonmaterial entity, the experience we call "self" is the natural by-product of the language-equipped brain's routine functioning. As we speak or think, we perform a measurable physical act whose products are at once displayed in the endogram, that is to say, registered in our consciousness. The products are the images and thoughts, on the one hand, and the sense of a self that is generating them, on the other. Whether we think or speak aloud, electrodes attached to the organs of speech, tongue, throat and lips, or fingers, hands and arms (in the case of sign-language speakers) will register the proprioception of the activity in progress. It is this proprioception that gives us the sense of authorship, the sense of an active "self." The upshot is that, besides the experience of what we are saying or thinking, we also experience that *we* are saying or thinking it. This awareness of a self is a real experience and the core around which our personality is built. What is not real is the illicit reification of our self-experience that turns the process into an intrapsychic agent. Though a blatant misconstruction, this latter is an important player in humanity's mythologies.

Looking at the role of the self, we find that with the passage of time it is increasingly enriched with our observations about our dispositions, preferences, and characteristics. Furthermore, these firm up into a consistent and predictable behavioral formula, a personality. With the self-experience as a core, we add to it the cumulative record of our past conduct and end up with a fairly accurate model of who we are. The model grows more distinct with time, more detailed, defended, and rationalized, and it has an ever increasing guiding influence on the brainstem's decision making. The way this works involves the generation of mental options that are congruent with the personality, so that the brainstem readily opts for what is being offered. In his foreword to Benjamin Libet's *Mind Time* (2004), Stephen Kosslyn depicts the circular relationship between personality and brainstem function in a most revealing way:

> "What one is" governs how one actually makes the decisions. And making that decision and experiencing the actual consequences in turn modifies "what one is," which then affects both how one constructs alternatives, rationales and anticipated consequences

Looking at the role of the self, we find that with the passage of time it is increasingly enriched with our observations about our dispositions, preferences, and characteristics. Furthermore, these firm up into a consistent and predictable behavioral formula, a personality.

and how one makes decisions in the future. Thus,
with time one's decisions construct "what one is."

To regard this carefully built and integrated existential entity as a mere social construct is, therefore, wide of the mark. This is not to say that there is no societally defined element in the edifice, as expressed in attitudes, choices, and culturally molded mindsets; but the final pattern of traits is concrete and personal. To label this product unreal or delusional, as some enthusiasts would, is as absurd as the other extreme, the view that the self is some form of spirit, soul, or nonmaterial manifestation.

The question of moral responsibility is a perennial one. To answer it is not difficult. The conscious mind, able to monitor itself and foresee outcomes, is responsible for the mental options it presents to the brainstem. These can be so drastic and overwhelming that the brainstem has no choice but to comply. History and even present-day events are replete with fanatics whose mindsets checkmate the brainstem and make martyrdom and death acceptable. Examples like these and manifestations of the will, so called, clearly indicate that mechanisms "to do one's thing" exist, and that although we are not free in the absolute or entelechy sense, we are responsible for our actions.

As for the onset of the conscious self, that is to say, the first appearance of an entity that is reflectively aware of itself, Antonio Damasio, in *Self Comes to Mind* (2010), observes:

How wonderful it would be to discover where and when the robust self came to mind and began generating the biological revolution called "culture." But in spite of the ongoing research efforts of those who interpret and date the human records that have survived time, we are not able to answer such questions.

On the strength of the data available to Damasio, what he says is correct, though not if we take the model that I am proposing into account. Although it is true that human records did not survive, the emergence of the "self" is easy to trace. It first appeared and became an identifiable experience when the brain gained voluntary motor access to itself, first to name, and later to speak and generate, the proprioception that is the self's experiential core. All the aspects of brain processing that were submerged before could now be labeled, thought, experienced, and handled by the language-wielding new subsystem, the mind. The link-up of Damasio's "robust self" with the mind is, therefore, as old as is the breakthrough to language, the event that turned the animal brain's awareness self-reflective and marked the emergence of *Homo sapiens*.

Turning to the changes that the acquisition of language instantiated, Damasio reflects on these changes in some detail:

To hold extensive memory records not only of motor-skills but also of the facts and events, in particular of personal facts and events, those that make up the scaffolding of biology, of personhood and the individual's identity, these depending on the ability to reconstruct and manipulate memory records in a working brain-space, parallel to the perceptual space, an off-line holding area where time can be suspended during a delay and decisions freed from the tyranny of immediate responses.

Damasio's list of what the breakthrough to language gave the brain—the workspace, the mind, the access to memory, the facility to control and organize, and all without response-compulsion—is not, however, matched by his reflections on consciousness. The contrast between the clarity of his views on language and the uncertainty about his views on consciousness has to do with the absence of a model that is able to show how the many aspects of the brain are related in forming an integrated system. To quote him further:

When we take the long view of the tree of life, we cannot fail to recognize that organisms do progress from simple to complex. In that perspective it is reasonable to wonder when consciousness appeared in the history of life. What did it do for life? If we

scan biological evolution as an unpremeditated
march up the tree of life, the sensible answer is that
consciousness appeared quite late, high in the tree.

Reading this passage, we cannot tell what Damasio means by the term "consciousness." Does he mean the uniquely human reflective state, or does he mean the nonreflective awareness of the animal brain? Either way there is a problem, for if he has the former in mind, then the claim that "consciousness appeared quite late, high in the tree" is imprecise. It is as if Damasio were reluctant to restrict reflective consciousness to *Homo sapiens* alone, but rather wants it to cover primates, cetaceans, and intelligent animal life-forms even further back in evolutionary time. This means that he seems to think of consciousness as a quality that came on gradually, rather than as a crisp and defining neurofunctional innovation that rewired the human brain and gave it leverage for self-handling.

If, on the other hand, he has the unreflective awareness of the infrahuman brain in mind, then the phrase "high in the tree" is even less appropriate. This is because awareness, the sensory representations that the motor system responds to, is no latecomer in biological evolution. Rather, in its simpler form it already existed in early multicellular organisms where information processing was integrated and centralized for the motor system to be effective. As we have seen in chapters 2 and 3, it is possible to trace the awareness phenomenon back to its phylogenetic roots by way of the reflexive response to the sensory spots of the primitive cell, whose "primitiveness" was already quite complex.

The failure to locate the onset of consciousness (as distinct from awareness), just like the failure to locate the onset of the "self" and of the mind (the language-controlled aspect of the brain), highlights the need for the model I am proposing, a model that integrates the disciplines of neuroscience, linguistics, and evolutionary biology into a single system. It can hardly be doubted that such a system is needed, that all these phenomena are intimately related and that this is essential to understand the world.

There is, of course, another way to approach the question of locating and identifying the conscious mind. It is the mystic take of the late Jesuit paleontologist Pierre Teilhard de Chardin (1959). It is worth quoting for its sonorous irrelevance, its lack of information, and its unintended but unavoidable message that we should seek reality, think straight, and avoid nebulous fancies when theorizing about consciousness:

> Refracted backward along the course of evolution, consciousness displays itself qualitatively as a spectrum of shifting hints whose earliest terms are lost in the night.

UNFINISHED BUSINESS: SKELETONS IN THE CLOSET

The philosophers, as we all know, just take in each other's laundry, warning about confusions they themselves have created in an arena bereft of both data and empirically testable theories.

—Daniel C. Dennett, *Consciousness Explained* (1991)

The aim of this book is to present a model that accounts for all aspects of human consciousness. It is to show the connectedness of these aspects and to prevent the entertaining of ideas that may make sense in isolation but not when seen in the context of the whole. The three ideas I explore in this chapter are costly diversions—"major misdirectors of attention" or "illusion generators," to borrow Daniel Dennett's words—and should be seen for what they are.

I start by taking a closer look at David Chalmers's so-called hard problem, the bastard offshoot of neuroscience, which, as we shall see, is neither hard nor a problem. It is at best a misunderstanding, an unintentional sleight of hand that is scarcely obvious enough to be detected. It takes the form of a rhetorical question: "Why is there subjective, conscious experience over and above the neural information processing that is its substrate?"

To illustrate the point that experience and conscious experience are different phenomena, Chalmers (1996) speaks of a hypothetical twin of his, who has the identical experience and the identical response to this experience as Chalmers himself but, unlike Chalmers, is not conscious of it. This has the absurd implication that to be conscious of an ongoing event makes no difference to one's response to it. It also means that we should regard consciousness as a passive and inconsequential epiphenomenon, a ghost without causal connectedness or causal significance to the organism on whom it piggybacks.

Let us look at the consequences of separating consciousness from the organism's experience. One implication is that the organism's information processing must be taken to be sufficient unto itself, which results in a mystery that requires a solution. Confirming this, Thomas Clarke (1995) observes:

> If experience is taken to be something over and
> above the neurally instantiated functions, something
> extra which accompanies them, the central mystery

becomes the explanatory gap between function and experience.

The picture is clear. Chalmers has generated a maze of misconstructions. To find a way out, he redefines consciousness as a cosmic principle alongside those of space, time, energy, and gravity and thus falls back on mind–body dualism. Unimpressed, however, Patricia S. Churchland (1997) notes that

> the only thing you can conclude from the fact that … consciousness is mysterious, is that we do not understand the mechanisms.
>
> Moreover, the mysteriousness of a problem is not a fact about the problem … it is an epistemological fact about us.

In summary, the "hard problem" arose when the automated reflexive response of the single-cell organism was superseded by the data-processing arrangements of the multicellular form—that is to say, when all the incoming sensory information was totalized in the endogram and a new decision-making function, able to evaluate the data, evolved to find the right response. The animal brain's sensory awareness and the human brain's reflective (conscious) awareness are, therefore, anything but optional extras on top of cortical functioning. They are the indispensable components of existence. They are the "display canvas" for the brainstem's selection of motor responses, whether the response is just on-line (as is the case with animals) or a mixture of on-line and off-line (as is the case with humans).

On balance, Chalmers's "hard problem" is a traceable misconstruction that arises out of a flawed model of consciousness and mind. The conclusion that consciousness is neuroscientifically intractable and that we need a cosmic principle to account for it is wrong. Patricia S. Churchland sums it up this way:

> The argument is obviously a fallacy: none of the tendered conclusions follow, not even a little bit. Surrounded with rhetorical flourish, much brow furrowing and hand-wringing, however, versions of this argument can hornswoggle the unwary.

She then adds: "From the fact that we do not know something, nothing very interesting follows—we just don't know." Regrettably, problems like Chalmers's "hard problem" tend to have a long half-life, generating ripples, calling for rebuttals, and taking up brain power that could be better employed.

Turning to the second of the controversial issues, that of "computer consciousness," I refer to an article in the *Weekend Australian* (May 23, 1998) entitled "It Thinks,

Therefore …," in which George Dyson, author of *Darwin among the Machines*, is quoted as saying that artificial life is likely to evolve on computer networks. "I am certain," he adds, "that machines can achieve consciousness; maybe it has happened already." Dyson's idea is not new. In his book *World Brain* (1938), H. G. Wells speaks of a widespread intelligence that is conscious of itself. In 1938, this seemed like fiction. Could our future computers turn it into fact?

Australian-born computer scientist Hugo de Garis (1998), heading the Brain Builder project at Kyoto University, Japan, takes the view that artificial intelligence could be constructed but that hyperintelligent computers would find no use for human beings. He adds:

> I think it would be tragic if humanity would decide for ever never to build artificial intellects. It would be a decision not to create the next superior species. On a cosmic scale that would be like bacteria never evolving into multicelled organisms and eventually into humans.

Other computer scientists feel less sanguine, recognizing that the power of the computer to perform certain tasks represents only a narrow aspect of what it means to be intelligent. Still, there is something like tacit agreement that no reason exists, at least in principle, why computers of the twenty-first century, if of superior design, could not be conscious. These machines, it is felt, would constitute a further advance in evolution, a new species, in fact. They would relegate us to the role that chimpanzees represent for us. They would be able to repair and reproduce themselves, to supplant us and eventually rule the world.

The source of this view is the radical wing of the artificial intelligence community, the functionalists who believe that consciousness is the natural by-product of a correctly run computer program. David Chalmers (1996) notes, for example: "Whether it is neurons or silicon chips that constitute a system, it is causal patterns among circuits that are responsible for the conscious experience that arises."

The trouble is that nowhere in these views is it stated what consciousness is. Is it the computer that is conscious or is it the unfolding program that is conscious of itself? To compound the difficulties, it is also claimed that the repeatedly rerun program is not only the source of consciousness, but will, in due course, interact with and modify the inorganic frame that houses the circuitry. This is self-contradictory, for on technical grounds alone the workability of an artificial circuit depends on its effective isolation from its physical frame, and this isolation would prevent the interactions that would be needed for reconstitution and change. These are serious problems to answer, not least on account of the computer's important

The computer's performance is the obvious extension of the human brain's motor capability. It is complementary to, and epistemologically on a par with, extensions to the sensory side of the brain, like the telescope and the microscope.

place in the cultural middle ground and its impressive range of capabilities.

Let us therefore take a closer look at the issue by examining three key terms: "computer," "computer performance," and "consciousness." What can we conclude about them and about possible misrepresentations of which, at first sight, we may be unaware?

Taking "computer" first, we find that this alleged source of machine-generated consciousness is not what it is cracked up to be. It is a mere effigy, an entity in name only. It is no more than a cleverly crafted artifact, one essentially indistinguishable from the raw material out of which it is manufactured. Its shape and working parts are designed to facilitate the intended function, the switching around of the circuitry in clearly defined ways. In short, the computer is not an organic entity but an icon. There is nothing computerish about its constituents. It was given the name "computer," as names are given to objects like a "brick," without there being anything brickish about that particular lump of burnt clay. In a very real sense there is no such thing as either a "brick" or a "computer," over and above the molecular constituents that form all objects. So, how might consciousness—or the ability to think—be reasonably attributed to mere agglomerations of material? The question is rhetorical, the claim unsustainable.

Nor is the case built on the second of the key terms, "computer performance," any more convincing. The computer's performance is the obvious extension of the human brain's motor capability. It is complementary to, and epistemologically on a par with, extensions to the sensory side of the brain, like the telescope and the microscope. Just as these sensory aids deepen our penetration by enabling us to see inside the cell and to detect invisible radio sources in distant galaxies, our digital computers empower us to process much of what used to be quite unimaginable or unthinkably complex.

Given this obvious parity between the sensory and the motor extensions of the brain, it is surprising that whereas no one would suggest that the electron microscope or the gamma ray detector can actually "see," or that these implements have vision, many in the artificial intelligence community believe that the computer's performance *is* thinking and that the processes involved generate real consciousness. This is to say that the computer is more than an aid for the brain, a claim that, though far-fetched, is not altogether surprising. This is because consciousness is a free-floating term that is often misused.

This leaves us with the third of the key terms, "consciousness," to look at and see whether we can make better sense of it in the context of computer functioning. If, as we have seen, the computer is a *pseudo-entity*, an artifact, we need to identify the critical feature that makes an organism a real entity, with consciousness as an integral part. The answer lies in the living organism's thermo-dynamic depth, the informational wealth that has been accumulating ever since the breakthrough to life, some 3.8 billion years ago. It was at that point that a self-supporting and self-enhancing biochemical formula emerged out of the prebiotic soup and began its progress toward ever-increasing complexity. The biochemical formula is expressed in the form of a continuous chain of carriers, that is, organisms with identical cellular fingerprints and a central data-processing center. This means that unlike computers, organisms are not agglomerates but ecosystems of coacting cells with a functional focus. In the course of evolutionary complexification of the living system, every modification was incorporated for the greater viability that resulted. The specialization of components followed and led to the upgrading of information processing on which survival depended. Therefore, from the moment of its inception, life was an intertwined system of cellular coprosperity, an orchestration of components and subcomponents into a single functional focus that stood for the system as a whole.

The living organism is the end product of eons' worth of painstaking construction, selected for and incorporated at every critical juncture. In light of the immensity of this edifice and the structural depth that consciousness represents, the computer, lacking cellular cohesion and intrinsic identity, is an absolute non-starter.

Finally, we come to the qualia, the concept which, according to Dennett (1991), does not constitute a valid refutation of physicalism because it is so confused that it cannot be put to any use or be understood in any noncontradictory way. Dennett is right; but might physicalism be used to pin down qualia and put an end to this perennial controversy?

The question to account for is this: how do the digital raw data of our nerve impulses end up as "qualia," that is, as the colors, sounds, tastes, smells, pain, and pleasure we actually experience? The trouble is that the bio-electric pulses the sense organs generate are nothing like the qualia we perceive; the transformation that converts the raw data into experience is far from clear. This results in a gap in our knowledge that can be used, and is being used, to advance the claim that qualia and qualia conversion are the work of some nonmaterial agency, like Descartes's *res cogitans*, the mind-half of dualism. To add weight to this point, it is also claimed that what person A sees as "red," person B may see as "blue," and vice versa, a claim that is difficult to refute. Likewise, the inaccessibility of the conversion of raw data to qualia makes it hard to prove that there is nothing nonmaterial about the process.

In spite of these difficulties, we have ways to solve the problem. The conversion of raw data into the qualia idiom is the conversion of digital into analog. It is an ingenious way of turning the unwieldy flood of incoming pulses into a user-friendly form, a kind of neural language. Thanks to it, the ocean of transverse and pressure waves in which the organism is immersed can be experienced as readily accessible continuous qualities, that is, as colors and sounds rather than pulses and vibrations. The qualia idiom is a practical solution to a biological problem. It is in universal use in nature for signaling and receiving information by flora and fauna alike. In light of this, the claim that qualia are the product of a nonmaterial (Cartesian) mind is wide of the mark.

To expand on this last point, consider what would be the case if the claim were correct that qualia were linked to *res cogitans*. Since, as we have seen, the whole biota works with the qualia idiom, we would have to assume that it is replete with *res cogitans*: birds and bees, insects and flowers, all with full-blown Cartesian minds to do their business—an unlikely scenario. On the other hand, and still with the assumption that the qualia are the products of minds (but minds are not possessed by flora and fauna), an even more absurd scenario would have to be faced. This is because transverse and pressure waves are all the biota could have, raw data of immense complexity, the meaningful and continuous processing of which would be impossible even to imagine. The conclusion is clear: qualia are not mind-linked, but are legitimate products of a biological process that renders information easy to handle and effective.

Let us, however, go a step further and show that person A's red qualia cannot look blue for person B, that perception is a lawful process and there is no room for fanciful anomalies. Consider the "Purkinje effect." Named after the nineteenth-century Austrian physiologist who undertook the study of color perception, it involves the gradual loss of color sensations as the level of illumination decreases. The process of dechromatization, the fading and vanishing of hues (at twilight, for example) is a function of the wavelength of the light involved. The least energetic, longer waves of "red" fade out first, followed by "yellow," "green," "blue," and finally by the most energetic, shortest wavelengths of "violet." The reemergence of color takes place in the reverse order when the gray light of early dawn turns gradually into full sunlight. Those who have experienced dusk or dawn in a garden or a forest will recall the effect—the turning on or off of the technicolor world at the start or at the end of the day.

As for the claim of seeing red where the color presented is in fact blue—and vice versa—it is significant that no qualia-swaps of any description are ever said to be taking place outside the visual range of the electromagnetic spectrum. The reason for this is not far to seek: all qualia experiences have close physical correlates, which, except for those in visual perception, can be easily checked for their accuracy. Nevertheless, even in this area where it is so easy to make dubious claims, there are ways of separating fiction from fact. The correlated sensations of heat and red light at one end of the spectrum and ultraviolet rays and violet light at the other end come at once to mind. The reason is that both heat and ultraviolet radiation generate qualia, that is, physical effects, which, owing to their correlation with red and violet respectively, render any claim of a "color-switch" untenable. This is because the heat-rash cannot be attributed to ultraviolet radiation, nor ultraviolet damage to red light. So even here in this fuzzy zone of verbal reporting, the game is up and hard facts prevail.

With illicit ideas out of the way and qualia being recognized as analog transforms of the digital substrate, why is there a measure of doubt and wonder about their source? The answer is that the human brain, but only the human brain, is able to generate qualia experience internally, though without knowing how this is done. It is, of course, through its language facility that it can access, recall, and reexperience sensations and perceptions that are stored in its memory. It can see colors, shapes, and all manner of things in its imagination and in the absence of external stimuli.

By contrast, the animal brain, lacking the off-line mechanism for accessing its stored sensations, can have qualia experience only through direct perception. It is able to see red only when there is something red to see. It is locked into having to react to the world, and as it has no off-line mechanism to generate internal (mental) experience it is not able to see or imagine what is not there.

However, in the absence of understanding of how the human brain generates qualia in intrapsychic space, those not acquainted with the system's intricacies can easily conclude that a nonmaterial (Cartesian) mind is at work. This conclusion is wrong, of course, but without a model to show how the mind-equipped brain works its magic from within, it can be perplexing indeed.

The resolution of such problems, even if complex, is, as we have seen, well within the reach of the thinking brain. Perhaps the hardest nut for it to crack is its own wondrously subtle functioning, though not even this exceeds its powers of decoding. In any case, if we are to give serious thought to its possible role in the evolutionary process, confusions about its identity and the misconstructions that go with it have to be eliminated. Only with these mental trip-wires out of the way can the conscious mind begin to think about its place in the scheme of things, where it is the highest expression of life, the ever-expanding eddy in the stream of entropy.

AT THE EDGE OF COMPREHENSION

As for belief, there are things as clear as the sky, yet men prefer to sit under an upturned barrel.

—Ko Fang (fourth-century natural philosopher, China)

Let us recap what this book has sought to accomplish, namely, the building of a model that accounts for the emergence of the human mind and its autonomous (free) functioning. To see what we would be up against without this model, I cite the opening passage of an article by the neuroscientist Christof Koch, entitled "Finding Free Will" (2012):

> In a remote corner of the universe on a small blue planet, gravitating around a humdrum sun in the outer districts of the Milky Way, organisms arose from the primordial mud and ooze in an epic struggle for survival that spans aeons. Despite all evidence

to the contrary, these bipedal creatures thought of themselves as extraordinarily privileged, occupying a unique place in a cosmos of a trillion trillion stars. Conceited as they were, they believed that they and only they could escape the iron law of cause and effect that governs everything. They could do this by virtue of something they called free will, which allowed them to do things without any material reason.

Can you truly act freely? The question of free will is no mere philosophical banter; it engages people in a way few other metaphysical questions do. It is the bedrock of society's notions of responsibility, praise and blame. Ultimately it is about the degree of control you exert over your life.

In terms of my model, this perspective is not justified. This is because free will, or at any rate its lawful variant, functional autonomy, was achieved by the "bipedal organism" courtesy of the very "iron law of cause and effect" the "conceited creatures" are supposed to have escaped. Indeed, it was the "iron law of cause and effect" that, by dividing the prebiotic causal chain, brought about life, generated the mind, and gave it a say in its own affairs. So let me outline how it happened and how we got where we are.

The breakthrough to *Homo sapiens* began with the neotenous regression to neuroplasticity at an ideal age for engaging the vocal medium in interpersonal manipulation. This resulted in the linkup of the speech areas with the motor cortex and led to the laying down of a new, off-line (intracortical) response mechanism. It is this off-line mechanism that enables the brain to access and handle its experience internally and manage its affairs.

The off-line mechanism generates language; language creates the organism's sense of self or agency, which is an integral feature of reflective functioning. As a result of language, human experience is always double stranded. It is comprised of what we experience and of the sensation that *we* are experiencing it. This brings on the oscillation of the attention between the two strands, a functional innovation that makes perseveration (the concentration on topics) possible in a "global workspace." Thanks to the global workspace, an extended time-span is now at the human brain's disposal, enabling it to collate and integrate disparate sensory information in the production of higher-quality behavior. It is a breakthrough into a world of consciously directed insightful behavior, a vital aspect of autonomous functioning.

The dramatic expansion and the qualitative upgrading of the human brain's powers alter the relationship between the cortex and the brainstem, the home of biological values and decision making. The language-using and thought-capable brain generates mental options for the brainstem in every instance. It is this contribution of the cortex that makes it an active partner in the Darwinian selection of behavior and in the shaping of the organism's fate. The brainstem still does the deciding, but the cortex is now able to load the dice with the options it offers up for selection and the bias this creates.

As for the human mind, it is a neural subsystem of the brain. Its tool is language, while its range and experience are defined by what language is able to access and handle. The mind is not a nonmaterial agency, but a physical entity, a subsystem that uses the same circuitry and brain processes that perception uses in registering and dealing with the world.

To summarize, all the phenomena of human experience are traceable expressions of the system and make sense only in terms of it. Thus, the *off-line mechanism* (our brain within our brain), the *mind module*, the *attentional oscillation*, and our *sense of agency* and *functional autonomy* (our free will) are no longer unconnected mysteries, but are achievements of the brain's emancipation into the world of knowledge and thought.

The work done, the system cleansed of false interpretations, we are free to look for the conscious mind's rightful place in the cosmic scenario. This is possible because the system is no longer side-tracked by self-generated misconstructions. Human emergence, which had its beginnings with the emergence of simple cells 3.8 billion years ago, is an awesome achievement, a triumph of life working

The mind is not a nonmaterial agency, but a physical entity, a subsystem that uses the same circuitry and brain processes that perception uses in registering and dealing with the world.

uphill against the entropic gradient. But what about the onset of life itself, the ancestral cell, the event that started everything? Was it a matter of chance that bordered on the miraculous, or was it one of inevitability? We have, as we shall see, enough evidence to hint at an answer.

Whether the breakthrough to the metabolizing and replicating first cell occurred on the planetary surface and was driven by solar energy or in deep sea hydrothermal vents where minerals for organic compounds were plentiful and conditions for biogenesis were favorable, the complexity of the first cell is staggering. Paul Davies, in his book *The Fifth Miracle* (1998), notes that

> the living cell is the most complex system of its size
> known to mankind. Its host of specialized molecules,
> many found nowhere else but in living material,
> are themselves enormously complex. They execute
> a dance of exquisite fidelity, orchestrated with
> breathtaking precision ... yet this is a dance with no
> sign of a choreographer, no intelligent supervisor, no
> mystic force, no conscious controlling agency.

As for its informational wealth, Richard Dawkins (1986) tells us that "each cell contains a digitally coded data-base, larger in information content than all thirty volumes of the *Encyclopaedia Britannica* put together."

This raises the question of how, since random chemical self-assembly could not have done it, such extraordinary organizational complexity was generated. While macro-molecules with crucial biological information to pave the way to life have been identified, the breakthrough must have occurred when, to quote Davies, "life opted out of the strictures of chemistry by employing an informational control channel to create a new, emergent world of autono-mous agency." The implication of this is far-reaching. "It is," writes Davies, "that the laws of nature encode a hidden subtext, a cosmic imperative to generate life and through life its by-products: mind, knowledge and understanding." It also implies that "the laws of the universe have engi-neered their own comprehension." Expressing the same idea, the distinguished biologist Christian de Duve (1995) points to the fact that "life is an obligatory manifestation of the combinatorial properties of matter," and that "life and mind emerged not as a result of freakish accidents but as a natural manifestation of matter written into the fabric of the universe."

Significant as these observations about the onset of life may be, the prebiotic side of cosmic evolution is no less impressive in its bio-friendly character. Indeed, the singu-larity's unfolding into the universe, all without external input or guiding corrections, is an unbelievably tight tra-jectory that led to the breakthrough to life. The constants of nature, the laws of physics, the accuracy of the strengths of the forces that guarantee the stability of matter, the steadiness of solar energy output, the availability of hydrogen fuel for aeons of time, all with near-zero tolerance for deviation—all of this boggles the mind. The enormous cosmic distances that shield quiescent regions from turbulent ones and the ubiquitous spin that keeps planets and stars in orbit and prevents gravitational collapse are no less amazing. It is this incredible precision of the parameters and of the laws of nature that underpin and guarantee the emergence of life that prompted the astronomer Fred Hoyle (1983) famously to remark, "The universe looks like a put up job." In a similar vein, Davies (1998), just as impressed by the chain of astronomically unlikely odds that had to come together to secure the prebiotic passage to life, notes: "The cliché, that life is balanced on a knife edge, is a staggering understatement. No knife in the universe could have an edge that fine."

By all indications, therefore, it seems that life is not the "the chemical scum on a moderately sized planet," the accidental impurity that, according to Stephen Hawking, many scientists take it to be, but something unique and significant. This is how de Duve (1995) characterizes what this uniqueness means:

> The contention that all living organisms derive from a common ancestor rests on overwhelming evidence ... all living organisms are constructed of the same

material, function according to the same principles and indeed, are actually related. All are descendants of a single ancestral form.

This means that although life is carried and represented by an endless series of organisms extant at any given time, the genome, the database, is an uninterrupted, single cosmic phenomenon. What is unique and important about life is that it breaks the causal monopoly that had ruled the prebiotic world. It does this because it is the source of an information-based second causation that organisms carry and implement. Consider, then, that during the prebiotic phase of the universe, from the big bang to the emergence of the ancestral cell, all changes were in accord with the laws of physics. It was a continuous unfolding of transformations with no agency to affect it in any way.

By contrast, under the new, life-augmented causal duopoly, no transactions in which living organisms participate are predictable by the laws of physics alone. Instead, they are now codetermined by the judiciously implemented information the increasingly evolved organisms possess and can activate. This is a drastic departure, one made possible by the mechanical leverage that the genome has evolved. What we have here is a defining point in cosmic evolution. Prior to it, the chain of causation went on inertially in domino fashion along the entropic (downward) gradient. Under the new dispensation, with life as a codeterminant, eddies are created in the stream of entropy, structures, information, and further enhancements to the system that does the enhancing.

Returning to where it all started, once life had gained a firm foothold in the ancestral cell, natural selection could take over and render the living forms increasingly diverse and complex. Through successive steps, this led to advanced information processing with awareness of decision making, and eventually to reflective consciousness and goal-directed behavior.

The organism's autonomous and knowledge-based functioning, and the causal leverage that goes with it, makes life an active player in evolution. So it may be of relevance that it does not incur thermodynamic debt of any kind. It may seem odd that this should be the case, for life does feed on energy, but not if we realize that what it uses is only waste energy. Indeed, the two billionths of the solar radiation the Earth captures each year, the source of the 150 billion tonnes of living matter, is energy the sun radiates away; it is not drawn by the Earth for that purpose. The implication of this is clear. Life on this planet, and on all planets that harbor life in the universe (billions of them, if life is written into the laws of nature), does not reduce the energy level of the cosmos. This may be significant, for should intelligent life here and elsewhere, with knowledge and the know-how to implement it, be playing a part in the cosmic story, its pro bono character could be decisive.

The aim of this book—the clarification of our human origins and the demonstration of the mind's physicality and causally autonomous functioning—leaves no gaps for gods or for mythological narratives. It clears the deck of misconstructions, traditional as well as new-fangled, so that we may assess our place in evolution in objective terms. The conscious living system, revealed for what it is, can now view itself against the background of its substrate, the amazing and rule-governed material universe. This is a challenging call. It is also the end of all the unanchored guesswork about free will (of the entelechy type) and about nonmaterial consciousness and the nonmaterial mind. Religions, unfazed by constraints of reality, just as much as erudite experts who try to explain mental phenomena with poised states between quantum coherence and decoherence, now have a traceable and consistent evolutionary explanation to confront.

"Life," writes de Duve, "is the most extraordinary adventure in the known universe, an adventure that has produced a species capable of influencing in decisive fashion the future unfolding of the natural processes by which it was born." The physicist Freeman Dyson (1988) goes a step further:

> It is conceivable, however, that life may have a
> larger role to play than what we have yet imagined.
> Life may succeed against all odds in moulding the

universe to its own purposes and the design of the inanimate universe may not be as detached from the potentialities of life and intelligence as scientists of the 20th century have tended to suppose.

Whether in agreement with most biologists and many physicists we take the achievement of life and consciousness to be an inevitable result of cosmic evolution or ascribe it to chance that borders on the miraculous, the clarification of murky and puzzling aspects of human functioning is essential. Items of fiction taken for facts subvert the quest to know the world and the self that knows. To end up with self-deception after 13.7 billion years of cosmic evolution from the big bang until now does no justice to the process that generated life. Life's causal powers, coupled with leverage and knowledge, is an inestimably important achievement, one whose implications and possible application should be a serious concern for all.

In the beginning there was the singularity, the point of infinite energy without time and space. This singularity unfolded and is now expressed in the universe, in life and in us, carriers of the genome, the informational core that prebiotic evolution has generated. The singularity is all that can be known; to reach beyond it even in thought is vanity. It is as if the mind could transcend its terms of reference, the conditions and constraints of its creation. As all thought is internal to the singularity, to speak of a creator that created it is to step outside the confines of what can be legitimately thought. Even if this were possible, it would be to exchange an immense subject one can study and try to understand for a featureless hypothesis we are in no position to contemplate. What then can we make of it? What can we make of the universe, the unfolded singularity, the immensity that engulfs us and of ourselves as part of the process? It is that we are expressions of an awesome and magnificent self-created and self-creating living system, an infinite existence. To find our place and role in it is a compelling task, challenge, and obligation.

GLOSSARY

Arborization
A branching tendency. In neurology, the dendritic growth of interconnections among neurons.

Association areas
Secondary or tertiary layers of the cerebral cortices overlapping primary maps and integrating inputs from different modalities. Mostly concerned with integrative and abstractive functions.

Australopithecus
Pleistocene ancestral protohuman, characterized by upright posture, human-like dentition, right-handedness as in humans, and cerebral development intermediate between apes and humans; estimated brain volume: 500 cc.

Auto-catalytic cycle
A self-enhancing and self-promoting state of a system.

Axon
The long process of a neuron that conveys impulses away from the body of the nerve cell.

Brain lateralization
The tendency to specialize and divide brain functions between the cerebral hemispheres.

Brainstem
The posterior part of the brain, structurally continuous with the spinal cord, usually described as including the medulla oblongata, the pons, and midbrain with its reticular formation.

Broca's area
A portion of the neocortex in the left hemisphere, tied up with the motor aspect of speech.

Central nervous system
Central aggregation of nerve tissue, consisting of the brain and the spinal cord in vertebrates.

Cerebral cortex
In humans and higher mammals, the large outer layer of the cerebral hemispheres; in large part responsible for our characteristic human behavior (see also *Neocortex*).

Cerebral hemisphere
Left and right portions of the cerebrum (see *Hemisphere*).

Cerebrum
Brain region, originating as bilateral swellings of the forebrain and ultimately forming the cerebral hemispheres.

Cognitive science
The systematic study of mental acts and processes by which knowledge is acquired. It combines branches of psychology with aspects of neuroscience, computer science, linguistics, and philosophy.

Collateral arborization
The postnatal neural branching development creating complex and interacting nerve nets.

Constancy mechanism
A neural device to compensate for apparent changes in the appearance of objects, allowing for their continued recognition.

Corpus callosum
The large bundle of nerve fibers that is the principal "cable" linking the left and the right hemispheres of the cerebral cortex.

Dendrites
Branch processes of neurons that synapse with axons and receive from them impulses, which they convey to the nerve cell.

Digital
Operating by the use of discrete signals to represent and handle data in the form of numbers or other characters.

DNA
Deoxyribonucleic acid: the genetic material of the cell, located in the nucleus.

Endogram
The brain's "situational statement" of what we are aware of at any given time; a construct denoting the brain's ongoing multimodal self-representation. Cognate with awareness, the endogram is the product of integrated experience in the brain.

Engram
The physiological memory trace recorded in the brain.

Entelechy
An uncaused causal agent; an autonomous source of causation.

Entropy
A measure of the disorder of a closed system, implying lack of pattern or organization.

Epigenesis
The widely accepted theory that an individual, animal, or plant develops through the gradual differentiation and elaboration of the fertilized egg cell.

Epistemology
The theory of knowledge, especially the critical study of its validity, methods, and scope.

Feedback (negative and positive)
The return of part of the output of an electronic circuit, device, or biological system to its input, so maintaining characteristics. In negative feedback, a rise in output reduces the input; in positive feedback, an increase in output reinforces input.

Forebrain
The most recently evolved part of the nervous system, subdivided into cerebral hemispheres and the thalamus.

Frontal evaluation cortex
Highest integrative center of the brain, collating information received from the sensory cortices for preparation of response.

Frontal lobes
The anterior region of the cerebral hemispheres.

Frontal scanning
Expression signifying the frontal lobes' filtering and generalizing function, resulting in the extraction of invariant features from processed experience.

Functional autonomy
The relative independence of a system or subsystem in maintaining its output and level of activity.

Global workspace
The reflective human brain's ability to access and integrate disparate sensory information off-line to generate higher-quality responses.

Gordian knot
A problem solvable only by drastic action.

Hemisphere
Either of the two cerebral hemispheres, the left or dominant, and the right or recessive hemisphere.

Holding mode
A neural technique that renders transient experience as if it were intransient, resembling a "still picture."

Homeostasis
The general capacity of living organisms to adjust to a chemical or physical stress by reestablishing equilibrium so as to preserve stable activity and composition.

Homo erectus
The immediate precursor of *Homo sapiens*, with wide geographical distribution (including Java man and Peking man). Brain volume: approximately 950 to 1,050 cc.

Homo habilis
East African protohuman tool-maker and tool-user; evolutionarily further advanced than *Australopithecus*. Brain volume: approximately 700 cc.

Homo sapiens
Modern human race, with brain volume of 1,350 cc, marked cerebral changes, neotenous development, much-increased frontal lobe participation, and articulated speech. Replaced Neanderthal subvariety that had larger overall brain size but less evolved frontal lobe functioning.

Homotopic sites
Contralateral areas of the brain that are mirror images of one another.

Imprint
Neurologically acquired and perpetuated fixed perception or disposition.

Indeterminacy
The impossibility of accurate knowledge or prediction.

Innervation
The supplying of sensory and motor nerves to an organ, incorporating it in an integrated larger network or system.

Laterality
Lateral specialization of the cerebral hemispheres. Used loosely, an asymmetry of the specialization.

Limbic areas
Evolutionarily ancient parts of the brain, concerned with emotions and instinctive behavior; connected with the hypothalamus and the lower brainstem.

Manipulo-spatiality
The skill of handling objects in the environment; hemispheric motor areas controlling it are understood to have been taken over by the speech areas in the left hemisphere for the purpose of language.

Midbrain
The middle region of the vertebrate brain between the hindbrain and the forebrain.

Natural selection
The principal method of biological evolution through the preferential survival and reproduction of organisms that are better adapted to their environment than their competitors.

Neanderthal
An extinct subspecies. See also *Homo sapiens*.

Negentropy (negative entropy)
A measure of order, structure, and organization, cognate with information and highly evolved systems.

Neocortex
The younger part of the outer surface of the cerebral hemispheres; thought to be involved in the highest cognitive functions.

Neotenous regression
The tendency in a species to exhibit increasingly incomplete structures and organizations at birth, allowing for postnatal neural growth.

Neoteny
Persistence of quasi-embryonic (uncommitted) features in the adult form of an animal.

Neuron
A nerve cell, the basic unit of the nervous system and the fundamental building block of the brain.

Nystagmus
A rhythmic oscillatory motion of the eye.

Objectification
The rendering of fluid and continuous variables, for example, in perception, into stable, objectlike fixed form.

Occipital lobes
The posterior part of the cerebrum, containing the areas of the brain concerned with vision.

Off-line
An internal loop operating in addition to the standard stimulus-to-response throughput.

On-line
The standard stimulus-to-response processing throughput.

Ontogeny
The development of an individual life history (as distinct from *phylogeny*, the evolutionary development of the species).

Paradigm
Any pattern or set of rules accepted as governing a field of knowledge.

Parietal lobes
Approximately the middle portion of each cerebral hemisphere, mostly concerned with somato-sensations and body schema.

Percept
An organized and integrated modality experience, for example, the stable appearance of a perceived object that can be identified and named.

Perceptual constancy
The neurofunctional device that maintains the invariant perception of objects, regardless of their apparent size, tilt, illumination, distance, etc.

Phase-transition
A point of abrupt qualitative change in a system's evolution, as when ice turns to water and water to steam in response to additional input.

Phoneme
Unit of speech sound; one of the set of speech sounds in any given language that serves to distinguish one word from another.

Phylogeny
The evolutionary relationships of a particular species.

Plasticity
The capability to be shaped or formed (especially neuro-developmentally) by the external environment.

Primates
An order of mammals; one of the taxonomic classifications of mammals that include lemurs, monkeys, apes, and humans.

Proprioception
One of the three sources of sensory input into the brain that conveys information about muscle activity and the state of the dynamics of the active body. The other two sources are *exteroception* (input from sense organs) and *interoception* (input from viscera and other internal structures).

Qualia
The subjective properties of color, sound, taste, smell, pain, and pleasure, rather than the neural events in the brain to which they refer.

Quantum leap
A discontinuous elevation or diminution of functioning on a higher plane or on a higher qualitative or energy level.

Referent
An object or event that words and percepts designate.

Reflective consciousness, conscious awareness
The human brain's capability to render its simple or animal awareness accessible and knowable to itself.

Representational cortices
Areas in the brain that deal with the perceptual integration of sensory inputs before their frontal evaluation.

Reticular activation system
A network of nerve fibers in the brainstem, the function of which is to activate portions of the cortex.

Salience
Significance or dominance of an element or point.

Scanning
The process of sifting data to extract invariant aspects and characteristics.

Schema (pl., *schemas* or *schemata*)
Complex internal representation, in part real, in part made up by the brain; a mental construct for evaluating and managing reality, which—though useful—is often a source of projective distortion.

Self-complexing
A system's ability to expand its structural and functional organization in terms of its own resources.

Semantics
The branch of linguistics concerned with meaning.

Short-term memory
Memory retained for brief periods of time, for example less than a day.

Singularity
A physical concept denoting a point or state in which the laws of physics that operate in a normally extended context no longer apply, and distortions or disappearance of parameters such as time and space can occur.

Solipsism
The condition where the self uses itself as the source for the purpose of proving itself or its beliefs.

Somatosensory
Referring to bodily sensation.

Supplementary motor areas
Structures on the superior surfaces of each of the cerebral hemispheres, thought to be the seat of the afferent to efferent transition (the point where the endogram links up with the motor system).

Synapse
The point where an electrical impulse is transmitted from one neuron to another.

Syntax
The branch of linguistics that deals with the grammatical arrangement of words.

Tachistoscope

An instrument used for the rapid presentation of visual stimuli to either the left or the right half of the retina in order to compare recognition thresholds of the cerebral hemispheres.

Taxonomy

The science and practice of classification.

Temporal lobes

Part of the cerebrum's lateral and frontal regions, which process the brain's auditory intake and take part in the decoding of language.

Thermodynamics

The branch of the physical sciences that is concerned with heat as a form of energy.

Vestigialized

Having attained a simple structure and a reduced size and function during the evolution of the species.

Visual cortex

The area at the back of the cerebrum responsible for the processing and inter-pretation of signals from the retinas (see *Occipital lobes*).

Volitional freedom

The assumed condition of being able to act without the constraints of causal determination.

Chapter 1

1. Functional autonomy is the relative independence of a system or subsystem in maintaining its output and level of activity.
2. An off-line mechanism is an internal loop that operates in addition to the standard stimulus–response throughput.
3. Entropy is a measure of the disorder of a system, implying lack of pattern or organization. Negentropy (or negative entropy) is a measure of order, structure, and organization.
4. Syntax is the branch of linguistics that deals with the grammatical arrangement of words.
5. The brainstem is the posterior part of the brain, structurally continuous with the spinal cord, which is usually described as including the medulla oblongata, the pons, and midbrain with its reticular formation.
6. Proprioception is one of the three sources of the sensory inputs into the brain conveying information about muscle activity and the dynamic state of the body. The other two sources are exteroception (inputs from sense organs) and interoception (inputs from viscera and other internal structures).
7. A singularity is a physical concept denoting a point or state in which the laws of physics that operate in a normally extended context no longer apply.

Chapter 2

1. Homeostasis is the general capacity of living organisms to respond to chemical or physical stress and to maintain equilibrium.
2. A phase-transition is a point of abrupt qualitative change in a system, for example, as when water turns to steam in response to additional input.
3. An on-line response is the standard stimulus-to-response processing throughput.
4. Saliences are the prominent features, the dominant stimuli, in the sensory representation that is the endogram.
6. An auto-catalytic cycle is a self-enhancing and self-promoting state of a system.

Chapter 3

1. A percept is an organized and integrated modality experience, for example, the stable appearance of a perceived object that can be identified and named.

2. Arborization is a branching tendency. In neurology, it refers to the dendritic growth of interconnections among neurons.

3. Manipulo-spatiality is the cortical ability to control the handling of objects in the environment.

4. Frontal scanning is the frontal lobes' filtering and generalizing function that results in the extraction of invariant features.

Chapter 4

1. Objectification is the rendering of fluid and continuous variables into stable, objectlike fixed forms.

Chapter 5

1. Epigenesis is the theory that an individual, animal, or plant develops through gradual differentiation.

2. Broca's area is the portion of the neocortex in the left hemisphere that is concerned with the motor aspect of speech.

Chapter 6

1. Nystagmus is a rhythmic oscillatory motion of the eyes.

2. A referent is an object or event that words and percepts designate.

3. Homotopic sites are contralateral areas of the brain that are mirror images of one another.

4. The global workspace is the reflective human brain's ability to prolong the time span between input and output to integrate disparate information.

5. The reticular activation system is a network of nerve fibers in the brainstem whose function is to activate portions of the cortex.

Chapter 7

1. A phoneme is a unit of speech sound: one of the set of speech sounds in any given language that serves to distinguish one word from another.

Chapter 8

1. A tachistoscope is an instrument used for the rapid presentation of visual stimuli.

2. An entelechy is an uncaused causal agent, an autonomous source of causation.

3. The association areas are secondary or tertiary layers of the cerebral cortices overlapping primary maps and integrating inputs from different modalities. They are mostly concerned with integrative and abstractive functions.
4. Collateral arborization is the postnatal neural branching development, creating complex and interacting nerve nets.

Chapter 9
1. Volitional freedom is the assumed condition of being able to act without the constraint of causal determination.

Chapter 10
1. The cortex is the outer layer of the cerebral hemispheres that is in large part responsible for human behavior.

FURTHER READINGS

Bickerton, D. 1995. *Language and Human Behavior*. Seattle: University of Washington Press.

Bickerton, D. 2009. *Adam's Tongue*. New York: Hill & Wang.

Churchland, P. S. 2011. *Braintrust: What Neuroscience Tells Us about Morality*. Princeton: Princeton University Press.

Churchland, P. S. 2013. *Touching a Nerve: The Self as Brain*. New York: W. W. Norton.

Damasio, A. 2010. *Self Comes to Mind: Constructing the Conscious Brain*. New York: Pantheon Books.

Davies, P. 2000. *The Fifth Miracle: The Search for the Origin and Meaning of Life*. New York: Simon & Schuster.

Deacon, T. W. 1997. *The Symbolic Species: The Co-Evolution of Language and the Brain*. New York: W. W. Norton.

Dawkins, R. 2009. *The Greatest Show on Earth: The Evidence for Evolution*. Ealing: Bantam, Transworld.

Dennett, D. C. 2003. *Freedom Evolves*. New York: Viking Press.

Donald, M. 1991. *Origins of the Modern Mind: Three Stages in the Evolution of Culture and Cognition*. Cambridge, MA: Harvard University Press.

Dyson, F. 1971. Energy in the universe. *Scientific American*, September. (Special issue on energy.)

Gould, S. J. 1977. *Ontogeny and Phylogeny*. Cambridge, MA: Belknap.

Kosslyn, S. M., W. Thompson, and G. Ganis. 2009. *The Case for Mental Imagery*. New York: Oxford University Press.

Libet, B. 2004. *Mind Time: The Temporal Factor in Consciousness*. Cambridge, MA: Harvard University Press.

Lieberman, P. 2006. *Toward an Evolutionary Biology of Language*. Cambridge, MA: Harvard University Press.

Luria, A. 1973. *The Working Brain: An Introduction to Neuropsychology*. Harmondsworth, Middlesex: Penguin.

Maynard Smith, J., and E. Szathmary. 2009. *The Origins of Life: From the Birth of Life to the Origins of Language*. Oxford: Oxford University Press.

Torey, Z. L. 2006. The immaculate misconception. *Journal of Consciousness Studies* 13 (12).

Torey, Z. L. 2009. *The Crucible of Consciousness: An Integrated Theory of Mind and Brain*. Cambridge, MA: MIT Press.

Tse, P. U. 2013. *The Neural Basis of Free Will: Criterial Causation*. Cambridge, MA: MIT Press.

Weinberg, W. 1978. *The First Three Minutes: A Modern View of the Origin of the Universe*. Glasgow: Fontana/Collins.

REFERENCES

Barrow, J. D., and J. Silk. 1984. *The Left Hand of Creation*. London: Heinemann.

Bickerton, D. 1995. *Language and Human Behavior*. Seattle: University of Washington Press.

Bickerton, D. 2009. *Adam's Tongue: How Humans made Language*. New York: Hill and Wang.

Bickerton, D., and E. Szathmary. 2009. *Biological Foundations and Origin of Syntax*. Cambridge, MA: MIT Press.

Blakemore, C. 1977. *The Mechanics of the Mind*. Cambridge: Cambridge University Press.

Blakemore, C. 1979. Representation of reality in the perceptual world. *CIBA Foundation Symposium* 69 (New Series): *Brain and Mind, Excerpta Medica*. Amsterdam: North Holland.

Blakemore, C., and S. Greenfield, eds. 1987. *Mindwaves: Thoughts on Intelligence and Consciousness*. Oxford: Blackwell.

Bronowski, J. 1977. *A Sense of the Future*. Cambridge, MA: MIT Press.

Brown, J. W. 1980. Brain structure and language production: A dynamic view. In *The Biological Studies of Mental Processes*, ed. D. Caplan. Cambridge, MA: MIT Press.

Bunge, M. 1979. The mind–body problem in an evolutionary perspective. *Brain and Mind. CIBA Foundation Symposium*, 69 (New Series): *Brain and Mind, Excerpta Medica*. Amsterdam: North Holland.

Buser, P. A., and A. Rougeul-Buser. 1978. Cerebral correlates of conscious experience. In *Proceedings of the International Symposium on Cerebral Correlates of Conscious Experience*. Amsterdam: North Holland.

Calvin, W. H. 1997. *How Brains Think: Evolving Intelligence Then and Now*. London: Weidenfeld & Nicolson.

Caplan, D., and N. Chomsky. 1980. Linguistic perspectives on language development. In *Language Functions and Brain Organisation*, ed. S. J. Segalowitz. London: Academic Press.

Chalmers, D. J. 1996. *The Conscious Mind: In Search of a Fundamental Theory*. New York: Oxford University Press.

Changeux, J. P. 1985. *Neuronal Man*. New York: Pantheon Books.

Chomsky, N. 1968. *Language and Mind*. New York: Harcourt Brace World.

Churchland, P. S. 1984. *Matter and Consciousness*. Cambridge, MA: MIT Press.

Churchland, P. S. 1997. The hornswoggle problem. In *Explaining Consciousness: The Hard Problem*, ed. J. Shear. Cambridge, MA: MIT Press.

Clarke, T. W. 1995. Function and phenomenology. *Journal of Consciousness Studies* 2(3).

Conway Morris, S. 2003. *Life's Solution: Inevitable Humans in a Lonely Universe*. Cambridge: Cambridge University Press.

Corballis, M. C. 1991. *The Lopsided Ape*. New York: Oxford University Press.

Creutzfeldt, O. D. 1979. Neurophysiological Mechanisms and Consciousness. *CIBA Foundation Symposium* 69 (New Series): *Brain and Mind, Excerpta Medica*. Amsterdam: North Holland.

Creutzfeldt, O., and G. Rager. (1978). Brain Mechanisms and the Phenomenology of Conscious Experience. In *Cerebral Correlates of Conscious Experience: Proceedings of an International Symposium* (No. 6). Amsterdam: North Holland.

Crick, F. 1982. *Life Itself: Its Origins and Nature*. London: Macdonald.

Crick, F. 1994. *The Astonishing Hypothesis*. London: Simon & Schuster.

Crick, F., and C. Koch. 1995. Are we aware of neural activity in primary visual cortex? *Nature* 375.

Damasio, A. 2010. *Self Comes to Mind: Constructing the Conscious Brain*. New York: Pantheon Books.

Darwin, C. 1974. *The Descent of Man*, rev. ed. Chicago: Rand MacNally.

Davies, P. 1983. *God and the New Physics*. Harmondsworth: Penguin.

Davies, P. 1987. *The Cosmic Blueprint*. New York: Simon & Schuster.

Davies, P. 1992. *The Mind of God: Science and the Search for Ultimate Meaning*. London: Simon & Schuster.

Davies, P. 1998. *The Fifth Miracle: The Search for the Origin and Meaning of Life.* New York: Simon & Schuster.

Davies, P. 2007. *The Cosmic Jackpot: Why Our Universe Is Just Right for Life.* New York: Orion.

Davies, P., and J. Gribbin. 1991. *The Matter Myth: Towards 21st-Century Science.* London: Viking.

Dawkins, R. 1986. *The Blind Watchmaker: Why the Evidence of Evolution Reveals a Universe without Design.* New York: W. W. Norton.

Dawkins, R. 2000. *The Ancestor's Tale: A Pilgrimage to the Dawn of Life.* London: Phoenix/Orion Books.

Dawkins, R. 2009. *The Greatest Show on Earth: The Evidence for Evolution.* Ealing: Bantam Transworld.

Deacon, T. W. 1997. *The Symbolic Species: The Co-evolution of Language and the Brain.* New York: W. W. Norton.

de Duve, C. 1995. *Vital Dust: The Origin and Evolution of Life on Earth.* New York: Basic Books.

de Garis, H. 1998. It thinks therefore. *New Scientist.*

Dennett, D. C. 1991. *Consciousness Explained.* Boston: Little, Brown.

Dennett, D. C. 1995. *Darwin's Dangerous Idea: Evolution and the Meanings of Life.* Harmondsworth, Middlesex: Penguin.

Dennett, D. C. 1996. Facing backwards on the problem of consciousness. In *Explaining Consciousness: The Hard Problem*, ed. J. Shear. Cambridge, MA: MIT Press.

Dennett, D. C. 2003. *Freedom Evolves.* New York: Viking Press.

Diamond, J. 1991. *The Rise and Fall of the Third Chimpanzee.* London: Radius.

Dirac, P. A. 1976. *Physics and Beyond.* Radio Canada International.

Donald, M. 1991. *Origins of the Modern Mind: Three Stages in the Evolution of Culture and Cognition.* Cambridge, MA: Harvard University Press.

Dyson, F. 1971. Energy in the universe. *Scientific American*, September. (Special issue on energy.)

Dyson, F. 1988. *Infinite in All Directions: Gifford Lectures*. New York: Harper & Row.

Dyson, F. 2000. *Origins of Life*. Cambridge: Cambridge University Press.

Edelman, G. M. 1987. *Neural Darwinism*. New York: Basic Books.

Edelman, G. M. 1992. *Bright Air, Brilliant Fire*. Harmondsworth, Middlesex: Penguin.

Eiseley, L. 1961. *Darwin's Century*. Garden City, NY: Anchor Books.

Fodor, J. 1976. *The Language of Thought*. London: Harvester.

Fodor, J. 1983. *The Modularity of Mind*. Cambridge, MA: MIT Press.

Gazzaniga, M. S. 1989. Organisation of the human brain. *Science* 1.

Gazzaniga, M., and J. Le Doux. 1978. *The Integrated Mind*. New York: Plenum Press.

Geschwind, N. 1980. Some comments on the neurology of language. In *The Biological Studies of Mental Processes*, ed. D. Caplan. Cambridge, MA: MIT Press.

Goldman, P. S. 1971. Functional development of the prefrontal cortex in early life and the problem of neuronal plasticity. *Experimental Neurology* 32.

Goldman-Rakic, P. 1990. The prefrontal contribution to working memory and conscious experience. In *The Principles of Design and Operation of the Brain. Experimental Brain Research*, Series 21, ed. J. C. Eccles and O. Creutzfeldt. Heidelberg: Springer-Verlag.

Gould, S. J. 1977. *Ontogeny and Phylogeny*. Cambridge, MA: Belknapp.

Gray, Jeffrey. 2004. *Consciousness: Creeping Up on the Hard Problem*. Oxford: Oxford University Press.

Griffin, D. R. 1982. Animal communication as evidence of thinking. In *Language, Mind, and Brain*, ed. T. W. Simon and R. J. Scholes. Mahwah, NJ: Erlbaum.

Guiard, Y. 1980. Cerebral Hemispheres and Selective Attention. *Psychologica* 46.

Hardcastle, V. G. 1995. *Locating Consciousness*. Amsterdam: John Benjamins.

Harth, E. 1983. *Windows on the Mind: Reflections on the Physical Basis of Consciousness*. New York: Quill.

Hassler, R. 1978. Interaction of reticular activating systems for vigilance and the truncothalamic and pallidal systems for directing awareness and attention under striatal control. In *Cerebral Correlates of Conscious Experience: Proceedings of an International Symposium* (No. 6). Amsterdam: North Holland.

Hawking, S. 1988. *A Brief History of Time*. London: Bantam Press.

Hofstadter, D. R., and D. C. Dennett. 1982. *The Mind's I: Fantasies and Reflections on Self and Soul*. Harmondsworth, Middlesex: Penguin.

Hoyle, F. 1983. *The Intelligent Universe*. New York: Holt, Rinehart & Winston.

Humphrey, N. 1984. *Consciousness Regained*. Oxford: Oxford University Press.

James, W. [1904] 2001. Does consciousness exist? In *How to Build a Mind*, ed. Igor Aleksander, *Maps of the Mind*, Steven Rose (gen. ed.). New York: Columbia University Press.

Johnson, M. 1987. *The Body in the Mind: The Bodily Basis of Meaning, Imagination, and Reason*. Chicago: University of Chicago Press.

Kauffman, S. A. 2008. *Reinventing the Sacred: A New View of Science, Reason, and Religion*. New York: Basic Books.

Khroustov, G. F. 1968. Formation and highest frontier of the implemental activity of anthropoids. In *VII International Congress on Anthropology, Ethnology, Science*, vol. 3, Moscow.

Kinsbourne, M., ed. 1978. *Asymmetrical Function of the Brain*. Cambridge: Cambridge University Press.

Kinsbourne, M. 1982. Hemispheric specialization and the growth of human understanding. *American Psychologist* 37.

Koch, C. 2012. Finding free will. *Scientific American Mind* 23 (2).

Kornhuber, H. H. 1978. A reconsideration of the brain-mind problem. In *Cerebral Correlates of Conscious Experience: Proceedings of an International Symposium* (no. 6). Amsterdam: North Holland.

Krantz, G. S. 1961. Pithecantropine brain size and its cultural consequences. *Man* 2 (103).

Lakoff, G. 1987. *Women, Fire, and Dangerous Things: What Categories Reveal about the Mind*. Chicago: University of Chicago Press.

Lakoff, G., and M. Johnson. 1980. *Metaphors We Live By*. Chicago: University of Chicago Press.

Langacker, R. W. 1990. *Concept, Image, and Symbol: The Cognitive Basis of Grammar*. New York: Mouton de Gruyter.

Leakey, R. E. 1981. *The Making of Mankind*. New York: E. P. Dutton.

Le Doux, J. E. 1986. Brain, mind, and language. In *Mind and Brain: Dialogues in Cognitive Neuroscience*, ed. J. E. Le Doux and W. Hirst. Amsterdam: North Holland.

Lenneberg, E. H. 1967. *The Biological Foundations of Language*. New York: Wiley.

Libet, B. 1978. Neuronal vs. subjective timing for a conscious sensory experience. In *Cerebral Correlates of Conscious Experience: Proceedings of an International Symposium* (no. 6). Amsterdam: North Holland.

Libet, B. 1990. Cerebral processes that distinguish conscious experience from unconscious mental functions. In *The Principles of Design and Operation of the Brain: Experimental Brain Research*, Series 21, ed. J. C. Eccles and O. Creutzfeldt. Heidelberg: Springer-Verlag.

Libet, B. 2004. *Mind Time: The Temporal Factor in Consciousness*. Cambridge, MA: Harvard University Press.

Lorenz, K. 1978. *Behind the Mirror: A Search for a Natural History of Human Knowledge*. New York: Mariner Books.

Luria, A. 1973. *The Working Brain: An Introduction to Neuropsychology*. Harmondsworth, Middlesex: Penguin.

Lyons, J. 1977. *Chomsky*. Hassocks: Harvester Press.

MacKay, D. M. (1978). What determines my choice? In *Cerebral Correlates of Conscious Experience: Proceedings of an International Symposium* (no. 6). Amsterdam: North Holland.

Marshall, J. C. 1980. On the biology of language acquisition. In *The Biological Studies of Mental Processes*, ed. D. Caplan. Cambridge, MA: MIT Press.

Mateer, C. A. 1983. Motor and perceptual functions of the left hemisphere and their interaction. In *Language Functions and Brain Organisation*, ed. S. J. Segalowitz. London: Academic Press.

Maynard Smith, J., and E. Szathmary. 1995. *The Major Transitions in Evolution*. Oxford: Oxford University Press.

Maynard Smith, J., and E. Szathmary. 2009. *The Origins of Life: From the Birth of Life to the Origins of Language*. Oxford: Oxford University Press.

Milner, B. 1978. Clues to the cerebral organisation of memory. In *Cerebral Correlates of Conscious Experience: Proceedings of an International Symposium* (no. 6). Amsterdam: North Holland.

Minsky, M. 1985. *The Society of Mind*. New York: Simon & Schuster.

Mithen, S. 1996. *The Prehistory of the Mind: A Search for the Origins of Art, Religion, and Science*. London: Thames & Hudson.

Monod, J. 1972. *Chance and Necessity: An Essay on the Natural Philosophy of Modern Biology*. London: Collins.

Mountcastle, V. B. 1979. An organising principle for cerebral function: The unit module and the distributed system. In *The Mindful Brain: Fourth Study Program of the Neurosciences Research Program*, ed. F. O. Schnitt and F. G. Worden. Cambridge, MA: MIT Press.

Mountcastle, V. B. 1990. The construction of reality. In *The Principles of Design and Operation of the Brain: Experimental Brain Research*, Series 21, ed. J. C. Eccles and O. Creutzfeldt. Heidelberg: Springer-Verlag.

Nagel, T. 1965. Physicalism. *Philosophical Review* 74:339–356.

Netley, C., and J. Rovet. 1983. Relationships among brain organisation, maturation rate, and the development of verbal and nonverbal ability. In *Language Functions and Brain Organisation*, ed. S. J. Segalowitz. London: Academic Press.

Oakley, D. A. 1985. Animal awareness, consciousness, and self image. In *Brain and Mind*, ed. D. A. Oakley. New York: Methuen.

Oakley, D. A., and L. C. Eames. 1985. The plurality of consciousness. *Brain and Mind*, ed. D. A. Oakley. New York: Methuen.

O'Keefe, J. 1985. Is consciousness the gateway to the hippocampal cognitive map? A speculative essay on the neural basis of the mind. In *Brain and Mind*, ed. D. A. Oakley. New York: Methuen.

Ornstein, R. E. 1972. *The Psychology of Consciousness*. San Francisco: Freeman.

Penrose, R. 1994. *The Shadow of the Mind*. London: Oxford University Press.

Pinker, S. 1994. *The Language Instinct: How the Mind Creates Language*. New York: Wm. Morrow.

Ploog, D. 1979. Phonation, emotion, cognition, with reference to the brain mechanisms involved. In *CIBA Foundation Symposium* 69 (New Series): *Brain and Mind, Excerpta Medica*. Amsterdam: North Holland.

Porter, G. 1971. *Molecules to Man*. London: Heinemann.

Posner, M. I. 1993. Seeing the mind. *Science* 262.

Premack, D. 1986. *Gavagai! or The Future History of the Animal Language Controversy*. Cambridge, MA: MIT Press.

Ringle, M. 1982. Artificial intelligence and semantic theory. In *Language, Mind, and Brain*, ed. T. W. Simon and R. J. Scholes. Mahwah, NJ: Erlbaum.

Rose, S. 1973. *The Conscious Brain*. London: Weidenfeld & Nicolson.

Sagan, C. 1977. *The Dragons of Eden*. New York: Random House.

Sagan, C. 1980. *Broca's Brain*. London: Hodder & Stoughton.

Schrödinger, E. 1967. *What Is Life? The Physical Aspects of the Cell, Mind, and Matter*. Cambridge: Cambridge University Press.

Searle, J. R. 1992. *The Rediscovery of the Mind*. Cambridge, MA: MIT Press.

Singer, I. B. 1991. *In My Father's Court*. New York: Farrar, Straus & Giroux.

Sommerhoff, G. 1974. *Logic of the Living Brain*. London: Wiley.

Sperry, R. W. 1976. A unifying approach to mind and brain: Ten-year perspective. In *Progress in Brain Research*, vol. 45: *Perspectives in Brain Research*, ed. M. A. Corner and D. F. Swaab. Amsterdam: Elsevier.

Springer, S. P., and G. Deutsch. 1981. *Left Brain Right Brain*. San Francisco: W. H. Freeman.

Stapp, H. P. 1996. The hard problem: A quantum approach. In *Explaining Consciousness: The Hard Problem*, ed. J. Shear. Cambridge, MA: Bradford Books, MIT Press.

Strawson, G. 1994. The impossibility of moral responsibility. *Philosophical Studies* 75 (1–2):5–24.

Strawson, G. [1998] 2011. Free will. In *Routledge Encyclopedia of Philosophy*, ed. E. Craig. London: Routledge.

Szentagothai, J. 1993. Self organization: The basic principle of neural functions. In *Theoretical Medicine 14*. Amsterdam: Kluwer Academic.

Teilhard de Chardin, P. 1959. *The Phenomenon of Man*. New York: Harper & Row.

Tennant, N. 1984. Intentionality, syntactic structure, and the evolution of language. In *Minds, Machines, and Evolution: Philosophical Studies*, ed. C. Hookway. Cambridge: Cambridge University Press.

Tobias, P. 1990. Some critical steps in the evolution of the hominid brain. In *The Principles of Design and Operation of the Brain: Experimental Brain Research*, Series 21, ed. J. C. Eccles and O. Creutzfeldt. Heidelberg: Springer-Verlag.

Torey, Z. L. 2009. *The Crucible of Consciousness: An Integrated Theory of Mind and Brain*. Cambridge, MA: MIT Press.

Trevarthen, C. 1979. The tasks of consciousness: How could the brain do them? In *CIBA Foundation Symposium* 69 (New Series): *Brain and Mind, Excerpta Medica*. Amsterdam: North Holland.

Weinberg, S. 1978. *The First Three Minutes: A Modern View of the Origin of the Universe*. Glasgow: Fontana/Collins.

Whorf, B. L. 1956. *Language, Thought, and Reality*. Cambridge, MA: MIT Press. Revised edition, 2012.

Wilson, E. O. 1978. *On Human Nature*. Cambridge, MA: Harvard University Press.

Wu, K. C. 1982. *The Chinese Heritage*. New York: Crown Publishers.

Zeman, A. 2009. *A Portrait of the Brain*. London: Yale University Press.

Zimmer, C. 2011. 100 Trillion Connections. *Scientific American*, January.

INDEX